Kauderwelsch
Vol. 46

Impressum

Bob Ordish
German — Word by word
published by
REISE KNOW-HOW Verlag Peter Rump GmbH
Osnabrücker Str. 79, D-33649 Bielefeld
info@reise-know-how.de

Revision Elfi H.M. Gilissen
Layout Kerstin Belz
Layout Conception Günter Pawlak, FaktorZwo! Bielefeld
Cover Peter Rump, Coverfoto: © Yuri Arcurs@Fotolia.com
Illustrations Bielefeld Marketing, Christine Schönfeld, Andreas Wagner
Print & Binding Werbedruck GmbH Horst Schreckhase, Spangenberg

ISBN 978-3-89416-036-4
Printed in Germany

This book is available in every bookshop in Germany, Austria,
Switzerland and Benelux. If you can't find it, please ask your
bookseller to order it from one of the distributors listed below:

Germany Prolit GmbH, Postfach 9, 35461 Fernwald (Annerod)
Switzerland AVA-buch 2000, Postfach 27, CH-8910 Affoltern
Austria Mohr Morawa Buchvertrieb GmbH
Sulzengasse 2, A-1230 Wien
Belgium & Netherlands Willems Adventure, www.willemsadventure.nl

www.reise-know-how.de

This book is accompanied by audio material
containing all words and phrases in this book,
spoken by a German native speaker.

Are you interested in becoming a Kauderwelsch author?
Take a look at
www.reise-know-how.de/rkh_mitarbeit.php

Kauderwelsch

Bob Ordish

German

Word by word

Reise Know-How
On the Internet
www.reise-know-how.de
info@reise-know-how.de

Up-to-date information, supplements after copy date, book shop, useful hints & special offers for travellers

This language guide is different!

Why? Because it enables you to actually speak the language and understand the people.

How? Apart from the things they have in common with any other language book such as vocabulary, model sentences, etc., the books in the Kauderwelsch series have the following special features:

They explain enough of the **grammar** in simple terms for you to get speaking right away without hours of drudgery, even if you're not word perfect.

All the examples used are translated twice: **word by word** and into proper English. The literal version shows you exactly how the sentence in the foreign language is constructed, the very basis of the language's structure. This is important because a language may have a completely different way of building sentences or mode of expression than English. Without a literal rendering, it's often virtually impossible to locate the function of individual words.

The **authors** writing for this series are travellers who've learnt the language in the country itself. So they know exactly what the people say in everyday life and how they say it. This is helpful, because a language as it is spoken is frequently much simpler and more direct than in literature.

Especially important in a country are **body language**, **gestures** and **rules of behaviour**. Without getting this right, even the best speaker will find it hard to make proper contact. That's why all the books in this series also focus on non-verbal communication.

These language guides aren't grammar books, but much more than a phrase book! They can help you, if you put in a little time and effort, to get a whole lot more out of your visit than a "speechless" tourist ever could.

Contents

Grammar

Conversation

Introduction

"There's no point learning German. They all speak English."

Well, yes and no – or **jein** as the Germans would say – **ja** + **nein**. On the one hand, it's true that particularly the young Germans do speak English – although less so in the area which used to be East Germany. There is no doubt that you can survive with English. But is that all you want? Even in Germany, a many people don't speak enough English to keep up a proper conversation and, even if your own German is limited, you'll get people on your side by at least making the effort. You'd be amazed how much goodwill – even a basic knowledge of German – is worth.

The language can seem pretty daunting at times, though, and the Germans themselves say: **Deutsche Sprache, schwere Sprache!** – "German language, difficult language!". Whereas, say, French or Spanish are relatively accessible to English-speakers because vocabulary and word order are so similar, German is usually entirely impenetrable to the uninitiated. This is because, although the two languages are both "Germanic" in origin, they have developed away from each other over the past several hundred years and been subject to different influences in that time. English also used to have a lot of the grammatical constructions I introduce in the first half of this book. They are long since gone. So too is a lot of the old Germanic vocabulary, gradually replaced by terms from the French, Latin, Greek or Italian. These are the reasons why, despite being Germanic, English nevertheless seems closer to the Romance languages.

One of the first things that will strike you is the length of many German words. At first, when you see the likes of **Selbstbestimmungsrecht**, you are likely to do a double-take. However, this is much less of a problem than you would think. It is just that German frequently joins words together which in English are written separately and, with experience, you learn where one word ends and the next one starts: **Selbstbestimmungsrecht**, "self-determination right" or, more correctly, "right of self-determination". A great help is that German is phonetic, i.e., it is spoken as it is written. Just think of what students of English have to go through when confronted with "bow", "bough", "though", "thought" and suchlike.
With German, once you've learned the rules, you'll always know how a word is pronounced, even if you've never seen it before.

A bigger problem is word order: German is written "the wrong way round". So much so that Mark Twain, the great American humorist, said that the language had to be read "in a mirror". Another memorable summing up, which I heard from a British soldier stationed in Germany, was that you "don't know till the end whether they're going to kiss you or kick you" – a reference to the verb often coming at the end of the sentence. The situation is, of course, more complicated than this. Suffice to say here that, with regard to word order, English and German really are very different. You will realize this just by looking at the examples later on, without my giving you every single rule which would defeat the object of this book.

The Peter Rump language learning technique, originally devised for German-speakers, is equally suitable for English-speakers wishing to learn German. The great strength of the system is that, by providing both a literal as well as a proper (in this case) English translation, it shows you exactly how the foreign language is built up. Since, as I said above, English and German sentence structure often differs so much, this technique is invaluable. Example:

Weißt du, ob sie schon angekommen sind?
know you whether they already arrived are
Do you know if they've already arrived?

Unless you wish to study German properly you won't master all the grammatical complexities. But that's not the aim of this book, which is simply to enable you to cope with some measure of success in the situations travellers find themselves in. If you are looking for an exhaustive account of German grammar, you will have to proceed beyond this book.

We have completely revised the book and adopted the new spelling effective since 1999. There have been ongoing discussions about the use of the spelling reform, **die Rechtschreibreform**, *and only the children are forced to learn the new spelling at school. The entire press has agreed on adopting the new rules only partially and ordinary people will remain writing the old way. So don't be confused, when you come across a different spelling – it is likely to be spelled according to the old rules.*

Also included is basic information on Germany, not only regarding accommodation, food, etc. but also the political system and German society. Even though it is so easy to travel to and around Germany these days, in many ways it is still something of a "mystery" country to the Anglo-Saxon world. Cultural links with France have always been much closer, and very many more English-speakers know French than German. It would also be naive to pretend that Germany has fully recovered its reputation among nations since the Nazi period and, although the vast majority of Germans now living had nothing to do with this, the country was until recently divided and militarily occupied as a direct result of it.

However, Germany isn't all fairy-tale castles, beer halls and boat trips along the Rhine. Without at least some knowledge of the language, and therefore the ability to raise yourself above the immediate tourist circuit, the essence of the country will pass you by.

Numbers

In order to make counting easier for you, every page has its number written in German.

Pronunciation & stress

The German alphabet is the same as the English plus some additional letters: **ä, ö, ß, ü.**

stress

The stem of the word is stressed, e.g. **geh**en in **gehen**, "go-to", i.e. "to go". Many prefixes, i.e. particles placed on the beginning of verbs such as **gehen**, are stressed: **aus**gehen in **ausgehen**, "out-to-go", i.e. "to go out"

pronunciation

consonants

b	**Bett** (bed)	as in English "**b**ed"
	ab (off)	at the end of a word or syllable like "**p**" as in "ma**p**"
c	**Celle** (a town)	like "**ts**" as in "le**ts**"
	Camping	otherwise like "**k**" as in "**k**ill"
d	**denken** (to think)	like "**d**" in "**d**ea**d**"
	Hund (dog)	at the end of word or syllable like "**t**" in ca**t**"
f	**folgen** (to follow)	as "**f**" in "to **f**ollow"

g	**geben** (to give)	as "**g**" in "to **g**ive", never "j" as in "**j**ump"
	Tag (day)	at end of word or syllable like "**ck**" as in "ba**ck**"
	heilig (holy)	preceded by **-i** at end of word, often a cross between "**ch**" in Scot. "lo**ch**" and "**h**".
	This sound is also often heard instead of"**ck**" *in words such as "Ta***g***" above.*	
h	**Hand** (hand)	as in "**h**and", never dropped –
	gehen (to go)	unless its purpose is to lengthen a preceding vowel
j	**ja** (yes)	German "jay" (yot), always like English "**y**" in "**y**es"
k	**Kern** (core, nuclear)	as in English "**k**iss", "**c**ore"
	Ecke (corner)	as in English, often written as "**ck**"
l	**Milch** (milk)	like English „**l**" but purer, never the dark "l" of the Southeast of England, which sounds more like a "w"
m	**Mutter** (mother)	like "**m**" as in English "**m**other"
n	**Name** (name)	like "**n**" in "**n**ame"

p	**Panne** (breakdown)	like "**p**" in "**P**aul"
q	**Quatsch** (nonsense)	as in English, always followed by "u"; not as in "queen" but "**kv**" as in "Ma**cV**itie"
r	**rennen** (to run)	in the South often similar to trilled **Scottish** "**r**"; in standard "High German" rolled at the back of the mouth, like **French** "**r**" but lighter
s	**Sonne** (sun)	before or between vowels like "**z**" in "**z**one"
	Haus (house), **Tasse** (cup)	At the end of a word or if doubled (= ss) like "**s**" in "**s**ave"
	Stadt (town, city) **springen** (to jump) **ist** (is), **Kasper** (Joker)	before "**p**" and "**t**" as "**sh**" in "**sh**all" if a word begins with this combination in the middle of a word like "**st**one" or "**sp**ider"
t	**Tasse** (cup)	like "**t**" in "**t**ooth"
w	**warten** (to wait)	like "**v**" in "**v**ery", not English "**w**"
x	**Hexe** (witch)	like English "**x**" in "inde**x**"
z	**Zigarette** (cigarette)	like "**tz**" in "Ri**tz**", not "z" as in "zebra"

consonantal combinations

ch	**Loch** (hole)	after a, o, u like "**ch**" in Scottish "lo**ch**"
	ich (I)	sometimes, especially after **i-**, like a cross between "**h**" and "**sh**"
	Wachs (wax)	before **-s** like "**x**" in "wa**x**"
ng	**singen** (to sing)	as in "**-ng**" in "si**ng**"
ph	**Philharmonie** (philharmonic hall)	"**ph**" as in English "**ph**ilharmonic"
sch	**Schiff** (ship)	like "**sh**" as in "**sh**ip"
ß	**Straße** (road, street)	**ß** = "ss" and is used to show that the preceding vowel is long, e.g. "shtrahsse"
ss	**Kuss** (kiss)	like "**ss**" in "ma**ss**es" The preceding vowel is short.
tsch	**Klatsch** (gossip)	like "**ch**" in "**ch**ur**ch**"

vowels

a	**Mann** (man)	short "**u**" as in Southern English "b**u**t"
	Sahne (cream)	long "**a**" as in "b**a**r" – often spelled **ah**
ä	**Städte** (cities)	short "**e**" as in "p**e**t"
	Fähre (ferry)	long as in "**ai**r" – often spelled **äh**
e	**Bett** (bed)	short "**e**" as in "b**e**t"
	lesen (to read)	long "**e**" similar to "**a**" in Northern English "g**a**te"
i	**ich** (I)	short "**i**" as in "f**i**t"; never as in "bite"
	ihr, **sie** (her, she)	long "**ee**" as in "b**ee**"; often spelled **ih**, **ie**
o	**Stop!**	short "**o**" as in "st**o**p"
	Ton (tone; clay)	long "**o**" similar to "**aw**" in "l**aw**n"; often spelled **oh**
u	**Kuss** (kiss)	short "**oo**" as in "b**oo**k"
	Buch (book)	long "**oo**" as in "f**oo**l"
ö	**östlich** (eastern)	short, cross between "**i**" in "d**i**rt" and "**eu**" in French "p**eu**"
	Öl (oil)	long
ü	**Glück** (luck)	short, like "**u**" in French "**u**ne" or English "d**u**ne", but with the lips pressed much closer together
	über (over, about)	long
y	**Mythos** (myth)	just like the long **ü** as above, not as in English "why"

diphthongs

(i.e. the adding of vowels together to form a different sound)

ai/ay	**Mai** (May)	English "**i**" as in "h**i**gh";
ay/ey		*are uncommon*
ei/ey	**beides** (both)	
au	**Sau** (sow, pig)	"**ow**" as in English "c**ow**"
äu/eu	**Gebäude**, (building) **Efeu** (ivy)	"**oy**" as in English "t**oy**"

Some useful words to start with

Below you find the most important phrases you'll need for a first conversation.

ja	yes
nein	no
Entschuldigung, ...	Excuse me, ...
danke	thanks

Wo finde ich ...?
where find I ...
Where is ...?

ein Hotel	a hotel
ein Taxi	a taxi
ein Restaurant	a restaurant
eine Tankstelle	a gas station
eine Toilette	a restroom
einen Supermarkt	a supermarket
einen Parkplatz	a parking space

The most important answers are:

nach links	to the left
nach rechts	to the right
geradeaus	straight ahead
zurück	back
an der Kreuzung	at the intersection
an der Ampel	at the lights

Some useful words to start with

Ich hätte gerne ...
I would-have like ...
I would like to have ...

einen Kaffee	a (cup of) coffee
ein Bier	a beer
ein Mineralwasser	a (glass of) mineral water
einen Fahrschein	a (tram, bus, train) ticket
ein Hotelzimmer	a hotel room
das (hier)	this, that

Was kostet/kosten ...?
what costs/cost ...
How much is/are ...?

When asking for the price you need to use the definite article instead of the indefinite. Substitute **einen** with **der**, **ein** with **das**, **eine** with **die**.

words you already know

Some German words still reveal the common Germanic origin of English and German: **Arm, Finger, Hand, Bier, Mann.** Besides **Kindergarten,** several German words have entered the English language in various fields, such as philosophy (*Immanuel Kant*) and psychology (*Sigmund Freud*):

Weltanschauung
Gestalt

There are also a number of "international" words which occur in many languages:

Bus	bus	**Taxi**	taxi
Sport	sport	**Theater**	theatre
Minister	minister	**Parlament**	parliament
Park	park	**Telefon**	telephone
Fax	fax	**Student**	student
Adresse	address	**Tourist**	tourist
Station	station	**international**	international

Station *here is used as in underground station.*
But: railway station = **Bahnhof.**

Still other words are quite similar to English, but not immediately recognizable:

Wein	wine
Hund	dog (hound)
Wald	forest (wold)

Word order – the simple sentence

German word order is often wildly different from English and very much a matter for the advanced student. However, you should be able to cope with simple sentences:

Subject	Verb	Object
Erich	**liest.**	
Erich	**liest**	**(eine) Zeitung.**
Erich	**liest**	**eine deutsche Zeitung.**
Erich	*reads*	*a German newspaper*
Erich	is reading	a German newspaper.

However, when time words are introduced, this order can change. Compare:

Er will Zeitung lesen und nicht ein Buch.
he wants newspaper to-read and not a book
He wants to read a newspaper and not a book.

Heute will er Zeitung lesen.
today wants he newspaper to-read
Today he wants to read a/the newspaper.

Er will heute Zeitung lesen.
he wants today newspaper to-read
He wants to read a/the newspaper today.

In more complicated sentences, many conjunctions "send the verb to the end" of the sentence.

Just by way of a sample:

not:
Sie war traurig, weil er konnte nicht kommen.

but:
Sie war traurig, weil er nicht kommen konnte.
she was sad because he not to-come could
She was sad because he couldn't come.

prefixes & suffixes

Prefixes are words or syllables placed on the front of a word to change that word's meaning, e.g. **pre**determine, **re**construct. English prefixes are very heavily influenced by Latin. German has a highly elaborate system of prefixes and it's not going too far to say that to really get to grips with the language you have to master them. Just look how they change the meaning of the simple verb **kommen**, "to come":

ankommen	to arrive
entkommen	to escape
bekommen	to get
vorkommen	to happen

Suffixes, placed on the end of a word, also tell you a lot about the word's function. The **-en** in **kommen** corresponds to English "to" in "to come". To stay with the example, the "**t**" in (**er**) **kommt**, "(he) comes", "is coming", tells us that this is the 3rd person singular. Other examples will be introduced as appropriate.

the articles: "the", "a/an"

Compared with German, English is gloriously simple here. German has retained many features which, in our own basically Germanic tongue, died out with the Anglo-Saxons. At this stage we'll keep it simple: The **indefinite article** "a/an" is **ein** or **eine** (French "un", "une"); the **definite article** "the" is **der**, **die** or **das** (French "le", " la") .

German therefore has three genders – masculine, feminine and neuter – whereas French has only two. You'll be learning more about gender, as well as how to use these articles, elsewhere in the book.

Nouns

Gender

As you've just learnt under "Articles", German has three genders: masculine (m), feminine (f) and neuter (n). Two things to note:

First, when learning a noun also learn the correct article with it, i.e. don't just learn **Schiff** (= ship), but **das Schiff** (= the ship).

Second, natural gender will often help you with grammatical gender, e.g. **die Frau** (= the lady), **der Mann** (= the man), but not always – **das Mädchen** (= the girl) is neuter.

By the way, you'll certainly have noticed by now that German nouns are capitalized = **groß geschrieben** ("large-written") and not **klein geschrieben**, ("small-written"), as in English. Some Germans would like to change this. The late **Bertolt Brecht**, the great dramatist, always wrote "small".

It would go well beyond the scope and aim of this book to give you a whole load of rules on this. If you follow the above advice and learn the article with the noun, you'll soon develop a feel for the right word for "the".

plural

You'll learn more about nouns in the section on grammatical cases.

Apart from exceptions such as "children", "oxen", "sheep" and a few others, all we do to form the plural in English is to add an -s onto the end of the noun. In German, the position is more complicated. Without going into this exhaustively, have a look at the following examples. Note that in the plural, the word for "the" is **die**, i.e. the same as the feminine singular:

das Getränk drink	**die Getränke** drinks
das Zimmer room	**die Zimmer** rooms
das Auto car	**die Autos** cars
das Glas glas	**die Gläser** glasses
die Zigarette cigarette	**die Zigaretten** cigarettes
die Warnung warning	**die Warnungen** warnings
der Stuhl chair	**die Stühle** chairs

Adjectives

In English you can say "blue sky", "a blue sky", "the blue sky", "the sky is blue" and the word "blue" never changes. In German this is not so because the adjective has to "agree" with the noun. This agreement depends not only on the position of, say "blue", but also on the gender of the noun it qualifies. Let's translate the above examples into German:

blauer Himmel
ein blauer Himmel
der blaue Himmel
der Himmel ist blau

Here, you see that with the definite article the masculine noun **Himmel** (= sky, heaven) requires the adjective to take the ending **-e** in the first example, an **-er** with the indefinite article or no article at all. Only when the adjective comes after the noun is usage as in English, with no change in the adjective.

feminine:	neuter:
schöne Frau/	**gutes Bier/**
eine schöne Frau	**ein gutes Bier**
die schöne Frau	**das gute Bier**
die Frau ist schön	**das Bier ist gut**
a/good-looking woman	a/good beer

comparison of adjectives

You'll be relieved to hear that English and German are very similar here although in the latter the comparative forms decline, i.e. "agree", just as do the adjectives:

schön	beautiful, good-looking, nice
schöner	more beautiful, nicer
der/die/das schönste	the most beautiful

die schönste Frau
the most-attractive woman

der schönste Mann
the most-attractive man

As in so many languages, the most frequently used adjectives tend to have irregular comparative forms:

Note that in the case of **groß**, *"big", "large", the comparative is not* "**großer**" *but* **größer**. *Remember,* **ein neuer Wagen** *does not mean "a newer car" but "a new car". "A newer car" is* **ein neuerer Wagen**.

gut	**besser**	**der/die/das beste**
good	better	best
viel	**mehr**	**der/die/das meiste**
much	more	most

Besides **schönste**, there is a still higher degree of comparison. You can say: **Claudia ist am schönsten** (literally: *"Claudia is at most-attractive"*), meaning "Claudia is the most attractive of them all".

When for comparison purposes we say "than", German uses **als** (it can also mean "as" and "when", depending on the context):

Heute ist es wärmer als gestern.
today is it warmer than yesterday
Today it is warmer than yesterday.

To express "as ... as", German says **so ... wie**.

Heute ist es so warm wie gestern.
today is it so warm as yesterday
Today is/it's as warm as yesterday.

If you want to say it's too warm, then quite simply:

Heute ist es zu warm.
today is it too warm
Today it's too warm.

Adverbs

In English these are formed by adding "-ly" to an adjective. German has no equivalent of this adverbial form in "-ly". German adverbs therefore look just like adjectives.

adjective:	adverb:
The waiter is quick.	The waiter works quickly.
Der Kellner ist schnell.	**Der Kellner arbeitet schnell.**

useful word pairs

gut – schlecht	good – bad
richtig – falsch	right – wrong
wahr – stimmt nicht	true – not right
immer – nie(**-mals**)	always – never
alles – nichts	everything, all – nothing
jeder – kein	every – no, none
jedermann – niemand	everyone – no one
hier – dort, **da**	here – there
schnell – langsam	quick, fast – slow
kalt – warm, **heiß**	cold – warm, hot
früh – spät	early – late
viel – wenig	much – little
groß – klein	big, large – small
zusammen – allein	together – alone
billig – teuer	cheap – expensive
preiswert – teuer	value-for-money – dear

Personal pronouns

The big difference from English is that German, like French and indeed most other languages, has more than one way of saying "you". There is a "polite" form, **Sie**, which you use with strangers clearly belonging to an age or social group different from your own; **du** (plural **ihr**), related to the defunct "thou" in English, is used in the family, between friends and young people in general.

However, there are gray areas, and it seems to me that even the Germans themselves are not absolutely certain which form to use in every situation. You are occasionally aware of a certain "fencing around" as they try to avoid committing themselves with a direct form of address. The situation you get to know the person in has a lot to do with it, e.g. you will almost certainly **duzen** ("use **du**") rather than **siezen** ("use **Sie**") your boss if you also happen to play in the same football team. The situation is, of course, similar to the French "vous" and "tu", although it's my impression that German is a little more formal here.

In full, the German personal pronouns are as follows:

Note that the meaning of **Sie** *(you),* **sie** *(she) and* **sie** *(they) is always clear from the context, even though they are pronounced identically.*

ich	I
Sie/	you *(formal, singular + plural)*
du	you *(familiar, singular)*
ihr	you *(familiar, plural)*
er	he
sie	she
es	it
wir	we
sie	they

Possessive pronouns

These must agree with the noun they qualify, e.g. **mein Buch** (my book), but **meine Frau** (my wife). The agreement can also change depending on whether the possessive pronoun comes before or after the noun, e.g. **das Buch ist meins**, as indeed it does here in English, too, ("mine"). With these considerations in mind, look at the basic forms of the German possessive pronouns:

mein	my	
Ihr/	your	*(formal, singular + plural)*
dein	your	*(familiar, singular)*
euer	your	*(familiar, plural)*
sein	his	
ihr	her	

sein	its	*(i.e. as with "his")*
unser	our	
ihr	their	*(i.e. as with "her")*

Examples of usage:

mein Freund (m)	my friend (boy-friend)
meine Freundin (f)	my friend (girl-friend)
mein Kind (n)	my child

seine Mutter	his mother
ihr Vater	her/their father
ihre Mutter	her/their mother
sein Kind	his child

meine, deine, seine, ihre, unsere, etc.

meine Freunde (m)	my friends (male)
meine Freundinnen (f)	my friends (female)
meine Kinder (n)	my children

seine Brüder	his brothers
ihre Brüder	her/their brothers
eure Bücher	your books
unsere Bücher	our books

To pluralize the possessive pronouns, just add **-e** *as with the singular feminine forms shown above.*

"To be" & "to have"

Later on you will see that English and German differ greatly in the way they form their tenses. **sein** (to be), not to be confused with **sein** (= his, its), and **haben** (to have) are central to the German tense system. This is why they are called "auxiliaries" – "helping" verbs.

The Germans also often use "to be" where an English-speaker might expect "to have". Take the English "I have come". In German this is **ich bin gekommen**, literally "I am come", which to us sounds rather Shakespearian.

Another point to note is that Germans almost always use this "I am" or "I have" form where we in English use the simple past. Therefore **ich habe gesagt**, which at first sight looks as if it means "I have said", is more accurately rendered simply by "I said".

sein and **haben** do not only have this auxiliary function. They are also verbs of full meaning, as in **Ich bin Arzt.**, (I am (a) doctor.) or **Ich habe eine Uhr.** (I have a watch.).

	sein *(to be)*	**haben** *(to have)*
ich	**bin**	**habe**
du	**bist**	**hast**
er/sie/es	**ist**	**hat**
wir	**sind**	**haben**
ihr	**seid**	**habt**
sie/Sie	**sind**	**haben**

Verbs

Basically, we can divide German verbs into two main types: weak and strong. Weak verbs add **-te** to their stem when forming the imperfect (i.e. past), e.g. **sagen** *(*to say), **er sagte** (he said). Strong verbs change the vowel of their stem, e.g. **singen** (to sing), **er sang** (he sang). Clearly, this is all very similar to English. The above German verbs conjugate "regularly" in the present tense:

	sagen *(to say)*	**kaufen** *(to buy)*
ich	**sage**	**kaufe**
du	**sagst**	**kaufst**
er/sie/es	**sagt**	**kauft**
wir	**sagen**	**kaufen**
ihr	**sagt**	**kauft**
sie/Sie	**sagen**	**kaufen**

Some verbs are slightly irregular:

	werden *(to become)*	**laufen** *(to run)*
ich	**werde**	**laufe**
du	**wirst**	**läufst**
er/sie/es	**wird**	**läuft**
wir	**werden**	**laufen**
ihr	**werdet**	**lauft**
sie/Sie	**werden**	**laufen**

Such verbs occur so frequently, however, especially **werden***, that you very quickly get used to these irregularities.*

modal verbs

There are six of these modal verbs, so-called because they "modify" the meaning of other verbs. Take the sentence **Er hilft ihr.** (He helps her.). This could be modified as follows:

Er kann ihr helfen.
He can help her.

Er muss ihr helfen.
He must help her.

This might look like pretty plain sailing, although the question of modal verbs is actually an involved one. They also frequently mean something different from what you might at first think:

	Er will ihr helfen.
not:	He will help her.
but:	He wants to help her.

Other modals:

dürfen (to be allowed to)

Sie dürfen hier nicht rauchen.
you allowed here not to-smoke
You're not allowed to smoke here.

mögen (to like; to want to)

Ich mag sie.
I like she
I like her.

Ich mag kein Bier trinken.
I like no beer to-drink
I don't want any beer.

sollen (to be meant to, to "ought" to)

Wir sollen helfen.
we are-to help
We're (supposed) to help.

können *(to be able, to "can")*	**müssen** *(to have to, to "must")*	**wollen** *(to want to)*
kann	muss	will
kannst	musst	willst
kann	muss	will
können	müssen	wollen
könnt	müsst	wollt
können	müssen	wollen

I've given you the forms of these modal verbs in detail because if you learn how to use the modal verbs you'll find your ability to express yourself in German increasing by leaps and bounds.

dürfen *(to be allowed)*	**mögen** *(to like, to want to)*	**sollen** *(to be meant to, ought)*
darf	mag	soll
darfst	magst	sollst
darf	mag	soll
dürfen	mögen	sollen
dürft	mögt	sollt
dürfen	mögen	sollen

The tenses

The past tense

*For those of you who know French, this is of course the same as the construction “**je suis allé(e)**” or “**j’ai trouvé(e)**”. The usage in the two languages is very similar. I should point out that my above remarks on the past tense are a simplification and there are certain cases where you would use the simple past. However, this is enough for your purposes at this stage.*

In English we use the simple past as a matter of course, i.e. “I went”. The precise German equivalent of this is **ich ging**. Germans rarely use this form in conversation. Instead, a German is likelier to say:

Ich bin nach Hause/ins Kino gegangen.
I am to home/in-the cinema gone
I went home/to the cinema.

Ich habe eine Kneipe gefunden.
I have a pub found
I(‘ve) found a pub.

This means you’ll have to learn the past participles of German verbs, i.e. **gesucht** (from **suchen** = to search), **gewartet** (from **warten** = to wait), etc. Some are, of course, irregular, e.g. **gemocht** from **mögen** = to like.

the future tense – the present tense

Usage in English and German differs here, too. In English we say “I’ll go” (the “ll” standing for “will” or “shall”, in itself a subject for the purists). The strict German equivalent of this is **ich werde gehen**. This, however, means rather “I will go” than “I’ll go” and, unless such emphasis is intended, Germans simply use the present tense when they mean the future. Take the following:

Ich gehe.

Depending on the context, this can mean either "I go.,I'm going., I'll go." Therefore, it is in fact only the context which can make clear what is meant:

Ich gehe sehr oft in die Kneipe.
I go very often in the pub
I go to pubs very often.

Ich gehe morgen schwimmen.
I go tomorrow to-swim
I'll go for a swim tomorrow.

negation

The simplest way of negating a statement in German is to place **nicht** (not) on the end of the sentence:

Ich kann.
I can
I can.

Ich kann nicht.
I can not
I cannot.

Ich rauche.
I smoke
I smoke.

Ich rauche nicht.
I smoke not
I don't smoke.

The German word order is reminiscent of an earlier stage of English, as in "tarry not", etc.

Questions

The following examples should make it clear how to form a simple question.

without a question word

statement:	question:
Morgen kommt er.	**Kommt er morgen?**
tomorrow comes he	*comes he tomorrow*
He's coming tomorrow.	Is he coming tomorrow?

statement:	question:
Er raucht.	**Raucht er?**
he smokes	*smokes he*
He smokes.	Does he smoke?

Basically, then, it's a matter of switching the position of the personal pronoun ("I", "you", "he" etc.) with that of the verb as well as raising the inflection of the voice.

questions & negation

Use **nicht:**

Kommt er nicht?
comes he not
Isn't he coming?

with a question word

Question words come at the beginning of the sentence:

Wer ist das? *who is that* Who is that?

wer?	who?	**wo?**	where?
wohin?	where to?	**woher?**	where from?
warum?	why?	**was?**	what?
wann?	when?	**wie viel?**	how much?

Remember that **wer** *does not mean "where" and* **wo** *does not mean "who". The word* **wohin?**, *"where to?", is comparable to the old English form "whither". Similarly* **woher?**, *"hither?", i.e. "where from?".*

was für ein? *what for a* what type of?

Word order in a German sentence using one of these question words is very different from English word order:

Was macht dein Freund?
what makes your friend
What does your friend do (i.e. job)?
What's your friend doing (at this moment)?

Woher kommt er?/Wo kommt er her?
where-from comes he/where comes he from
Where's he from (i.e. is he British, etc.)?
Where's he come from (e.g. today)?

Conjunctions

These little words help you link ideas together and produce more complicated sentences:

und	and
aber	but
sondern	but, on the contrary
oder	or
weil	because
da	because, since
wenn/falls	when, whenever/if
dann	then (after)
damals	then, at that time
entweder ... oder	either ... or
dass	that (relative pronoun, "I hear that she's here.")
ob	if

Ich habe eine Schwester und einen Bruder.
I have a/one sister and a/one brother.

However, use of most of these conjunctions involves a complication typical of German which you have already met: they "send" the verb to the end of the sentence:

Ich glaube, dass dort ein Hotel ist.
I believe that there a hotel is
I believe, there's a hotel over there.

By the way, where English often leaves out "that", as in the above example, German always puts in **dass**.

Da es regnet, bleibe ich zu Hause.
because it rains, remain I at house
Because it's raining I'll stay at home.

Erst möchte ich fernsehen*, dann können wir spazieren gehen.
first like I to-watch-TV, then can we to-walk to-go
I'd first like to watch TV. Then we can go for a walk.

* **fernsehen =** *literally "to see distantly'" also the literal meaning of our own, Greek-derived "television". Similarly* **Fernsprecher**, *"distant speaker", although this has been all but eliminated by the instantly recognizable* **Telefon**.

Prepositions

These are words such as "to", "for", "with" indicating direction or method. Use of German prepositions is closely linked to the question of grammatical case which, in English, ceased to be a problem hundreds of years ago. Therefore, not only do you need to learn that the word for "for" is **für**, but also that **für** takes the direct object or accusative case.

Other German prepositions, such as **an**, "on", "to", can differ in the case they take depending on their meanings and the context. This is very much a matter for the more advanced learner, and you certainly don't need to learn all the details unless you want to study German seriously.

But you should at least be able to recognize what's going on (for this you'll need to read the next chapter as well). Therefore, for each preposition I give the case or cases it takes:

accusative or direct object case

durch	through	**durch die Stadt** through the town
für	for	**für den Mann** for the man
ohne	without	**ohne mich** *without me* "count me out"
bis	till, up to	**bis jetzt** *up-to now* so far

dative, indirect object or "to" case

aus	out of, from	**aus Frankreich** *out France* from France
bei	near, by, at someone's place (French "chez")	**bei dir/euch/Ihnen** *by you/you/you* at your place
mit	with	**mit ihm/ihr** with him/her
nach	to	**nach Köln** to Cologne
	after	**nach mir** after me

von	from	**nicht weit von hier** not far from here
	by	**von meiner Mutter gemacht** *by my mother made* made by my mother
zu	to	**ich komme zu dir** *I come to you* I'll come over, etc.

prepositions taking either case, depending on meaning

in	in, into	*acc.*	**Er ging in das Haus.** He went into the house.
		dat.	**Er war in dem Haus.** He was in the house.
über	above, about	*acc.*	**Wir haben über den Berg gesprochen.** *we have about the mountain spoken* We talked about the mountain.
		dat.	**der blaue Himmel über dem Berg** the blue sky above the mountain

You'll have noticed such words as **den** and **dem** being translated as "the", as are the **der**, **die**, **das** you've already learned; so what's going on?

The cases

If you've studied Latin, you'll already know what to expect here. If not, you may find the idea of grammatical case pretty hard to grasp at first.

In English, we use prepositions plus word order to express the relationships between words. In German, much of this function is performed not only by prepositions but also by the grammatical cases, of which there are four (some other languages have even more). You learned right at the start that the word for "the" depends on gender, e.g., **der Mann**, **die Frau**, etc. Well, the form for "the" also changes to denote grammatical case.

Ich suche den Eingang.
I search the entrance
I'm looking for the entrance.

Here, **der Eingang** has become **den Eingang** to denote that **Eingang** is a masculine noun in the accusative, or indirect object case. Similarly, the indefinite article also changes from **ein** to **einen**, and any adjectives used also take this **-en** ending:

Ich suche einen billigeren Parkplatz.
I search a cheaper parking-space
I'm looking for a cheaper parking space.

For the feminine and neuter genders, however, there is no such change in this accusative case:

Ich sehe die schöne Frau.
I see the attractive lady.

Ich sehe ein junges Kind.
I see a young child.

These genders therefore remain just as you have already learned.

With the indirect object or dative case, though, all genders change. It will help you to think of this case as the "to" case, as expressing movement from a to b, even if this is sometimes rather abstract.

m	**Er bietet dem/einem Mann seinen Platz an.** *he offers to-the/to-a man his seat on* He offers his seat to the/a man.
f	**Er hält der/einer Frau die Tür auf.** *he holds to-the/to-a woman the door open* He is opening the door for the/a lady.
n	**Er gibt dem/einem Kind ein Stück Schokolade.** *he gives to-the/to-a child a piece chocolate* He is giving the/a child a piece of chocolate.

Masculine **der, ein** *and neuter* **das, ein** *change to* **dem, einem,** *and feminine* **die, eine** *change to* **der, einer**.

Adjectives in this case take **-en** for all genders, just as in the masculine direct object case: **dem alten Mann**, **der schönen Dame**, **dem jungen Kind**, as well as **einem guten Mann**, etc.

The **possessive** or **genitive case** is no longer used much in spoken German, although you should be able to recognize it:

m	
das Fenster des Busses *the window of-the bus* the bus window	**die Frau eines Mannes** *the wife of-a man* a man's wife
f	
der Schlüssel der Tür *the key of-the door* the door key	**der Mann einer Frau** *the husband of-a woman* a woman's husband
n	
die Lobby des Hotels *the lobby of-the hotel* the hotel lobby	**die Mutter eines Kindes** *the mother of-a child* the mother of a child

Here, then, masculine **der**, **ein** and neuter **das**, **ein** become **des**, **eines** (notice also the **-es** ending of **Mannes**, **Kindes**) and feminine **die**, **eine**, become **der**, **einer**, as with the direct object, dative case. Again, as in the dative, all adjectives in the genitive take the ending **-en**.

However, as I said above, this genitive case is not used much in spoken German, especially the **des** and **eines** forms, perhaps because they rather grate on the ear. Instead, other structures tend to be used in conversation:

die Frau von dem Mann	**dem Mann seine Frau**
the wife of the man	*to-the man his wife*
the man's wife	the man's wife

This latter example using the dative case, though frowned upon by purists, is frequently heard, especially in the southern half of Germany.

Also possible are:

Bernds Vater	**der Vater von Bernd**
Bernd's father	*the father of Bernd*
Bernd's father	Bernd's father

Your head's probably reeling after this section. You certainly won't take in all this information in one sitting. To recap, look at the following table.

normative or subject case
who? what? (who, what is?)

der gute Freund; der große Hund
the good friend; the big dog

die alte Kirche; die neue Hose
the old church; the new trousers

das schöne Mädchen; das bunte Bild
the pretty girl; the coloured picture

accusative or direct object case
who? what? (what do I see?)

f., n. identical to the above

den guten Freund; den großen Hund
the good friend; the big dog

Dative or indirect case/"to" case
who to? what to? (to whom do I give sth.?)

dem guten Freund; dem großen Hund
to-the good friend; to-the big dog
the good friend; the big dog

der alten Kirche; der neuen Hose
to-the old church; to-the new trousers
the old curch; the new trousers

dem schönen Mädchen
to-the pretty girl
the pretty girl

Object pronouns ("me, him", ...)

1st, 2nd person

In English we can say "give me the book" or "she sees me every day" and the word "me" does not change. In German, these sentences would be:

Gib mir das Buch. **Sie sieht mich jeden Tag.**

There are, then two forms – the dative, indirect object form **mir**, which really means "to me", and the accusative, direct object form **mich**. Similarly:

Ich gebe es dir.	**Ich habe dich gesehen.**
I give it to-you	*I have seen you*
I'll give it (to) you.	I saw you./I've seen you.

There is no such change with **uns** ("us"):

Er hat uns geschrieben.
He has to-us written.
He's written to us. / He wrote us.

Er hat uns gesehen.
he has us seen
He saw us. / He's seen us.

For the polite form of address, **Sie**, there is the indirect object form **Ihnen**, (for **sie**, "they", the form **ihnen**):

Object Pronouns ("me", "him", etc.)

Ich kenne Sie schon.
I know you already
We've met before.

Some verbs, such as **helfen** *("to help"),* **sagen** *("to say") take the indirect object, dative case.*

Ich würde Ihnen gerne helfen.
I would to-you like to-help
I'd like to help you.

The familiar plural form of address does not change:

Wir möchten euch was sagen.
we would-like to-you what to-say
We'd like to tell you something/talk to you.

Euch will ich nicht sehen.
you want I not to-see
You I don't want to see.

3rd person

Sie liebt ihn.
she loves him
She loves him.

Sie hilft ihm.
she helps to-him
She helps him. / She'll help him.

Er liebt sie.
he loves she
He loves her.

Er hilft ihr.
he helps to-her
He helps her. /He'll help her.

Kennst du das Buch?
know you the book
Do you know the/ this book?

Ja, ich kenne es.
yes I know it
Yes, I do (know it).

Kommen sie heute?
come they today
Are they coming today?

Er fährt jetzt zu ihnen.
he drives/travels now to them
He's going over to their place now (etc.).

That isn't quite the end of the 3rd person, though. Instead of the personal pronoun Germans often use the corresponding form of the definite article, e.g. **Der ist in Ordnung, der Karl.** ("Karl's a good bloke."), etc., instead of: **Er ist in Ordnung ...** The above examples, then, could also look like this:

ihn:	**Sie liebt den.**
ihm:	**Sie hilft dem.**

sie:	**Er liebt die.**
ihr:	**Er hilft der.**

sie:	**Kommen die heute?**
ihnen:	**Er fährt jetzt zu denen.**

denen *is the dative plural form of* **dem**, **der**, **dem**.

I wouldn't advise beginners to actually use these colloquial forms since they do require a fair amount of **Sprachgefühl** (= feel for the language). I just want you to be able to recognize them, since they crop up all the time.

Here & there

Hier and **dort** (or **da**). But that's not all. In English we used to have such words as "hither", "thither" and "whither". "Whither goest thou?" Answer: "Thither", i.e. "there", "to there".

While modern English makes do with "here" and "there", German still operates with "thither" and "hither", **hin** and **her**. Thus "come to me" is not **komm hier** but **komm hierher**, which is almost always shortened to **komm her**. Similarly, "I'm going there" is not **Ich gehe dort** but **Ich gehe dorthin** or simply **Ich geh' hin**.

hin and **her** crop up all the time with many different verbs. Correct usage is sometimes as much a matter of **Fingerspitzengefühl** (*"finger-tips-feeling"* = feel for the language) as purely grammatical logic.

"filler words" – schon, doch, noch, mal

You will notice these words coming up in conversation all the time, and correct usage of them is essential to mastering colloquial German. They do not only provide padding but also have concrete, "dictionary" meanings:

Es ist schon acht Uhr.
It is already eight o'clock.

Es ist schon ganz gut.
it is already quite good
Actually, that is quite good/a good idea, etc.

Es war doch gut.
it was still/however/even-so good
It was okay after all/it was good, etc.

Kommst du nicht mit?
come you not with?
Aren't you coming with me/us?

Doch!
of-course
Of course I am. / Yes, of course.

Es ist noch zu früh.
It is still too early.

Noch ein Stück, bitte.
still a piece, please
Another one/One more, please.

Gucken wir (ein)mal.
look we once
Let's see. / We'll just have to see.

Sag mal, wer ist der Typ da!
say once who is the guy there
By the way, who's that bloke there!

Die Lage ist doch noch zu retten.
the situation is even-so still to to-save
We can still save the situation even now.

Numbers

The German numbers seem fairly daunting at first since not only are they written as one word without hyphens but they are also the "wrong way round", i.e. instead of, say, "twenty-five" Germans say "five-and- twenty", a form virtually never used in English nowadays. This is something you just have to get used to. After all, for a traveller, numbers are one of the most important parts of a foreign language.

Note that "one", when it stands alone, is **eins** *(indef. article:* **ein, eine***), or at the end of a compound number:* **hunderteins***, 101; on the phone, and very often in conversation, you will hear* **zwo** *instead of* **zwei***, "two".*

0	**null**	10	**zehn**
1	**eins**	11	**elf**
2	**zwei (zwo)**	12	**zwölf**
3	**drei**	13	**dreizehn**
4	**vier**	14	**vierzehn**
5	**fünf**	15	**fünfzehn**
6	**sechs**	16	**sechzehn**
7	**sieben**	17	**siebzehn**
8	**acht**	18	**achtzehn**
9	**neun**	19	**neunzehn**

20	**zwanzig**	40	**vierzig**
21	**einundzwanzig**	50	**fünfzig**
22	**zweiundzwanzig**	60	**sechzig**
30	**dreißig**	70	**siebzig**

100	**hundert/einhundert**
101	**hunderteins**
102	**hundertzwei**
185	**hundertfünfundachtzig**
200	**zweihundert**

1000	**tausend/eintausend**
5000	**fünftausend**
1m.	**eine Million (1 Mio.)**
1bn.	**eine Milliarde (1 Mrd.)**
1 trillion	**eine Billion**

compound numbers

thousands	hundreds	units	tens

25 **fünfundzwanzig**
694 **sechshundertvierundneunzig**
3,278 **dreitausendzweihundertachtundsiebzig**

By the way, instead of "3,278" Germans – and indeed all other Continental Europeans – write "3.278". Our decimal point in, "1.5", is in German "1,5". In numbers , therefore, English and German usage of full-stops and commas ist the exact opposite.

ordinals

1st:	**erster**, **erste**, **erstes**; **der/die/das erste**
2nd:	**zweiter**, etc.
3rd:	**dritter**
4th:	**vierter**

10th:	**zehnter**
21st:	**einundzwanzigster**
100th:	**hundertster**

When used adjectivally, the German ordinals agree with the noun they qualify.

Es ist mein erster Besuch in Deutschland.
it is my first visit in Germary
This is/It's my first visit to Germany.

Telling the time

Wie spät ist es?
how late is it
What's the time?

Wie viel Uhr ist es?
how-much clock is it
What time is it?

Hast du/Haben Sie eine Uhr?
have you a watch
Do you have a watch?

Es ist ... It's ...

... eins/ein Uhr.
it is one/it is one clock
... one o'clock.

... fünf vor zwei.
... five before two
... five to two.

... viertel nach sechs.
... quarter after six
... quarter past six.

Note:
Es ist halb neun.
it is half nine
It's half past eight.

Whereas we think of the half-hour as coming after the previous full hour, for Germans it comes before the next one.

In order to express the time using numbers, Germans use a colon inbetween hours and minutes.

The 24-hour clock is used just where you would expect and, if anything, rather more often than in English-speaking countries:

Der Zug kommt um 22:11 (zweiundzwanzig Uhr elf) an.
the train comes at 22.11 hours in
The train arrives at 22.11.

kommt ... an
from **ankommen** *(to arrive). This is a "separable verb", in which the prefix ends up at the end of the sentence in certain circumstances. It would be beyond the scope of this book to go into detail.*

the Date – das Datum

Der wievielte ist heute?
the how-much is today
What's the date today?

Den wievielten haben wir?
the how-much have we
What's the date?

Es ist der erste August.
it is the first August
It's 1st August.

"1987" looks horrific at first, but it's easy enough to separate the component parts of this **Bandwurmwort** *(= "tape-worm-word").*

Wir haben den 1. August.
we have the 1st August
It's 1st August.

1987	**neunzehnhundertsiebenundachtzig**

months – Monate

Juni *is sometimes spoken and written* **Juno** *to avoid confusion with* **Juli**; **Juli** *is sometimes spoken* **Julei** *to avoid confusion with* **Juni**.

Januar	January	**Februar**	February
März	March	**April**	April
Mai	May	**Juni**	June
Juli	July	**August**	August
September	September	**Oktober**	October
November	November	**Dezember**	December

im Januar in January etc.

days of the week – Wochentage

Montag	Monday
Dienstag	Tuesday
Mittwoch	Wednesday
Donnerstag	Thursday
Freitag	Friday
Samstag	Saturday
Sonntag	Sunday

am Montag on Monday

Samstag *can also be* **Sonnabend** *(especially in the north and east of Germany).*

public holidays in Germany

There are more of these than in Britain or the United States, especially in the more Catholic parts of Germany such as Bavaria (**Bayern**) or Rhineland-Palatinate (**Rheinland-Pfalz**).

Neujahrstag	New Year's Day
Fasching/ Fastnacht	Shrovetide celebrations (especially in Mainz, Cologne, Düsseldorf)
Ostern	Easter
Karfreitag	Good Friday
Pfingstmontag	Whit Monday
Tag der Arbeit	May Day
erster Weihnachtstag	Christmas Day
zweiter Weihnachtstag	Boxing Day
Silvester	New Year's Eve, Hogmanay

Besides these there are also a lot of other, religious public holidays.

times of day – Tageszeiten

der Morgen	morning
(**morgen**)	(tomorrow)
Mittag	midday
(**der Mittag/ das Mittagessen**)	(lunch)
der Nachmittag	afternoon
der Abend	evening
die Nacht	night

time – Zeit

die Stunde	hour
der Tag	day
das Wochenende	weekend
morgens	in the morning
nachmittags	in the afternoon
nachts	at night

heute	today
tagsüber	during the day
vor zwei Tagen	two days ago (not: for two days!)
noch	still (etc.)
manchmal	sometimes
sofort	immediately
rechtzeitig	punctually, in time
die Minute	minute
die Woche	week
das Jahr	year
mittags	noon, at lunchtime
abends	in the evening
gestern	yesterday
morgen	tomorrow
bis morgen	till tomorrow; by tomorrow
schon	already (etc.)
noch nicht	not yet
immer	always
gleich	at once
spät	late
plötzlich	suddenly

the seasons – Jahreszeiten

der Frühling	spring
der Sommer	summer
der Herbst	autumn
der Winter	winter

im Frühling in spring etc.

im = in dem *(= "in the"). It's a matter of some subtlety to know when to use the contraction* **im,** *similarly* **ins** *for* **in das.**

Saying "Hello" & "Goodbye"

Guten Tag.
good day

"Good day", yes, except that, unless you're Australian ("G'day!"), you probably never say this. A more accurate translation, then, would probably just be "Hello!". There are no such problems with the following:

Guten Abend.	**Gute Nacht.**
Good evening.	Good night.

By the way, **guten** not **guter**, since **Abend** and **Tag** are regarded as being in the accusative, direct object case.

The German for "Goodbye" you almost certainly know already but, just for the record, here it is: **Auf Wiedersehen!** meaning, literally: "to (our) again-seeing". But what you'll hear at least as often, if not more so, is the little word **Tschüs!** or **Tschüss!** which is sometimes pronounced without "s" and an elongated "ö"– **Tschööö!** It is a less formal way of saying goodbye which is not only used by young people anymore. A lot of people even say **Tschau!** which is just the German spelling for the italian **Ciao!**.

Also used is **Mach's gut!**, meaning "all the best", etc. It literally means "do it well", and

Kauderwelsch Pronunciation Trainer

If you would like to hear the most important English sentences in this book from a native speaker, your bookshop can supply you with the Pronunciation Trainer for the book. It is also available from our Internet shop ***www.reise-know-how.de*** *All sentences in the book which can be heard on the* ***Kauderwelsch Pronunciation Trainer*** *are marked with an* 👂*. You can find out more about the Pronunciation Trainer on page 158.*

you might get the humorous response **Mach's besser!**, "do it better". Incidentally, you'll also occasionally hear **Bye!** or **Bye-bye!** in Germany – probably as all over the world – especially if the person you're talking to knows you're an English-speaker. Here are some other useful phrases:

Wie geht's?
how goes it
How are you?/How's things?

Wie geht's! *= short for* **Wie geht es dir?**, *polite form* **Wie geht es Ihnen?** *(both literally: "how goes it to-you"). Like the French "Comment ça va?"*

Bis nachher!
till afterwards

Bis später.
till later

Bis gleich.
till right-away
See you in a minute.

Gleich!
right away, coming

Gleich! *is often said by a waiter who then promptly disappears.*

Bis bald!
till soon
See you soon.

introductions

Das ist (die) Gabi.
that is (the) Gabi
This is Gabi.

Germans don't always say "the" Gabi, but it is a commonly used colloquial expression.

Freut mich, ich bin/heiße Bob.
pleases me, I am/called Bob
Pleased to meet you, my name is Bob.

Mein Name ist Jürgen.
my name is Jürgen
My name is Jürgen.

Ich bin (die) Monika.
I am (the) Monika
I'm Monika.

Ich darf bekannt machen.
I may known-make
Let me introduce you.

Angenehm.
pleasant
Delighted.

Es freut mich, Sie kennen zu lernen.
it pleases me, you know-to-learn
I'm pleased to meet you.

comprehension

Sprechen Sie Deutsch?
to-speak you German
Do you speak German?

... Englisch?
... English
... English?

... Französisch?
... French
... Französisch?

You will also hear:

Können Sie Deutsch?
to-be-able you German
Can you speak German?

Spricht/kann er Spanisch?
speaks/can he Spanish
Does/can he speak Spanish?

Ich verstehe.
I understand
I understand.

Ich verstehe nicht.
I understand not
I don't understand.

Note the following idiom:

Ich verstehe nur Bahnhof.
I understand only station
I don't understand a word.

Würden Sie bitte langsamer sprechen?
would you please slower speak
Would you speak more slowly, please?

Was heißt "car" auf Deutsch?
what calls "car" in German
What's the German for "car"?

A small conversation

Sind Sie zum ersten Mal hier?
are you to-the first time here
Is this your first visit?

Sind Sie alleine?
are you alone
Are you alone?

Wir machen hier Urlaub.
we make here holiday
We're on holiday here.

Ich bin mit Freunden zusammen hier.
I am with friends together here
I'm here with friends.

Ich bin hier zusammen mit meiner Frau/meinem Mann.
I am here together with my wife/my husband
I'm here with my wife/husband.

Gefällt es dir/Ihnen hier?
likes it to-you (familiar/polite) here
Do you like it here?

Wo kommt ihr her?/Woher kommt ihr?/ Von wo kommt ihr?
where come you (fam. pl.) from/where-from come you/from where come you
Where are you from?/Where do you come from?

Ich komme aus Australien.
I come out Australia
I come from Australia.

Ich bin Engländer/Engländerin.
I am Englishman/Englishwoman
I'm English.

Ich bin aus Irland.
I am out Ireland
I'm from Ireland.

Meine Frau ist Amerikanerin.
my wife is Americanwoman
My wife's an American.

Welche Staatsangehörigkeit haben Sie?
which nationality have you
What's your nationality?

Was sind Sie von Beruf?
what are you of profession
What (work) do you do?

Ich bin Lehrer/Lehrerin.
I am teacher (m/f)
I'm a teacher/I teach.

Ich bin Student/Studentin.
I am student (m/f)
I'm a student.

You can frequently form the feminine in this way by adding an **-in**.

Ich studiere noch.
I study still
I'm still studying (at university or college).

invitations

You'll be struck by the spaciousness and even opulence of many German homes, no matter if it is a **Neubau** *("new building", built after WWII) or in* **Altbauten** *("old buildings", built before the war) which mostly have been renovated expensively, since after WWII there were not many buildings left over in those beautiful architectural styles from past centuries. Germans love lots of plants, and the order and tidiness –* **Ordnung und Sauberkeit** *– is no mere cliché, in my experience even in student* **Wohngemeinschaften** *(literally: "living communities", but basically meaning "flat shares") or* **Studentenwohnheime** *("halls of residence").*

If you're invited to somebody's home for a meal, the following few items will come in handy:

Guten Appetit!
good appetite
Enjoy your meal!
(French: Bon appetit!)

Sehr lecker!
very tasty
Delicious!/Excellent!

Wie schmeckt es?
how tastes it
How does it taste?

Tu dir keinen Zwang an.
do to-you no compulsion
Don't stand on ceremony.

Danke, ich schaffe nichts mehr.
thanks, I manage nothing more
Thanks, but I really couldn't manage it.

Ich platze gleich.
I burst immediately
I'm stuffed to the gills, etc.

Ich habe schon genug getrunken.
I have already enough drunk
I've had enough to drink, thanks.

Ich muß noch fahren.
I must still to-drive
I still have to drive.

relations

das Ehepaar	married couple
der Ehemann/Mann	husband
die Ehefrau/Frau	wife
die Freundin	girlfriend
der Freund	boyfriend
der/die Verlobte	fiancée / fiancé
der Vater, Vati, Papa	father, dad, pop
die Mutter, Mutti, Mama	mother, mum, mom
der Bruder	brother
die Schwester	sister
die Geschwister	brothers and sisters
der Junge	boy
das Mädchen	girl
der Großvater, Opa, Opi	grandfather, grandad
die Großmutter, Oma, Omi	grandmother, grannie
die Tante – der Onkel	aunt – uncle
der Enkel	grandson
die Enkelin	granddaughter
der Neffe – die Nichte	nephew –niece
der Schwager	brother-in-law
die Schwägerin	sister-in-law

die Freundin *can also be a female friend;* **der Freund** *can also be a male friend.*

General expressions of politeness

To start with a general observation, you will find that Germans are rarely as effusively polite as many British or Americans. Germans have told me that when travelling in say, Britain, they are struck by this immediately. Some love it, others find it rather overwhelming.

In Germany, you'll find the people perfectly helpful, if a little cooler than you might be used to. In, for instance, shops, the expressions of politeness used may sometimes seem somewhat abrupt when translated into English. You can say, for example, **Ich bekomme ...** or **Ich krieg' ... ,** literally meaning "I get", but equivalent to our "Could I have ..., please". So in a pub you can hear:

Ich krieg' ein Bier.
I get a beer
A beer, please.

But you will not hear this in classy restaurants. As far as I can judge, though, no offence is ever meant or taken. The literal translation is clearly no guide at all to the true meaning of the words.

bitte is one of the most important expressions of politeness:

Können Sie mir bitte sagen, wo der Bahnhof ist?
to-be-able you (polite) to-me please to-say, where the station is
Excuse me, could you tell me where the station is, please?

Könnten Sie mir bitte zeigen, wie ich zum Bahnhof komme?
to-be-able you to-me please to-show, how I to station come?
Could you show me the way to the station please?

Bitte.
please
That's okay.

Bitte schön.
please nice
You're welcome.

bitte *has a variety of meanings. For instance, with the next old lady you offer a seat to on a German bus you can rattle off a quick* **Bitte sehr!** *(***sehr** *= very), meaning here: "Take a seat!"*

General expressions of politeness

The correct answer when being offered something is always:

Danke.	**Danke schön.**
thanks	*thanks nice*
Thanks.	Thank you.

The following are used pretty much interchangeably. You can use these when accidently bumping into someone, trapping onto his toe. But these are also used to ask for directions:

German **man** *(don't confuse it with* **der Mann**, *"the man") is like French "***on***". Strictly speaking it means "one", but since this tends to sound very much like the "royal we", it is usually better to adapt the translation to the context – "I", "we", "is it allowed to", etc.*

Verzeihen Sie! / Verzeihung!	**Entschuldigen Sie! / Entschuldigung!**
forgive (you)	*pardon (you)*
Excuse me!	Excuse me!

smoking or non-smoking

Darf man hier rauchen?
may one here to-smoke
Can I smoke/is it allowed to smoke here?

Bitte sehr!
please very
Please do! Go ahead!

Nein, hier darf man nicht!
no here may one not
No, it's "No Smoking" here!

Lieber nicht.
rather not
I'd rather you didn't.

Useful interjections

Ja! Jawohl!	That's right! / Yes indeed!
Freilich!	Of course! *mostly used in Bavaria*
Wirklich?	Really? You don't say!
Gut! Okay!	Good! / Fine! / Right! / O.K.!
(Wie) Schade!	(What a) pity/shame!
Nochmal, noch einmal!	Again, once more!
Ich weiß.	I know.
Das weiß ich schon.	I already know that.
Wem sagst du das?	You don't need to tell me!
Schon gut!	That's O.K.! / Forget it! / Don't worry!
Na und?	So what!

exclamations

Mein Gott!	My God!
Meine Güte!	My goodness! Goodness me!
(**Ja**) **doch!**	Oh yes (it is)!
(**Nein**) **doch!**	Oh no (it's not)!
Los, auf!	Get a move on! Step on it!
Mensch!	For God's sake! *(literally: "human being")*
O Mann!	Damn! Blast! What a pain!
Pech!	Bad luck! Tough!
Ach (**nein**)**!**	Oh (no)!
Ach ja!	You don't say! **Ach ja!** *can also express ironic disbelief.*
Schweinerei!	What a (bloody) mess! That's disgusting! Disgraceful!
So eine Frechheit!	What a damn cheek!
Scheiße!	Shit! Sod it!, etc.
Schitt!	*slightly less strong, than* **Scheiße,** *heard in the North*

The weather

As in all countries (not just Britain!), the weather is a frequent topic of conversation. Neither is the weather in Germany any better than Britain's, despite the propaganda. I know this from hard experience.

Wie ist das Wetter?
how is the weather
What's the weather like?

Es regnet.
it rains
It's raining.

Es gießt.
it pours
It's pouring.

Heute ist es sehr schön.
today is it very nice
It's a nice day today.

Schon wieder so ein Scheißwetter!
already again such a shit-weather
It's shit weather again./
It's a bloody awful day again.

Die Sonne scheint.
the sun shines
The sun's shining.

Das Wetter ist schrecklich.
the weather is terrible
The weather is terrible.

Accommodation – Die Unterkunft

If you aren't going to be staying in expensive hotels, there are plenty of other possibilities: **Pensionen**, **Gasthäuser** and, in the South, you will frequently see the sign **Fremdenzimmer** (*literally: "strangers' room"* – "room free/vacancies"). There is also a network of youth hostels (**die Jugendherberge**). These are often located near the centre of major cities. They are mostly frequented by school classes and it's advisable to phone through your booking a day or two in advance.

hotels, hostels, etc.

das Hotel	hotel
das Badezimmer	bathroom
das Gepäck	baggage
die Dusche	shower
der Schlüssel	key
das Bett	bed
die Etage/der Stock	floor
das Licht	light
die Tür	door
das Fenster	window
die Toilette	restroom
der Flur	corridor
der Fernseher	TV
die Minibar	minibar
das Doppelzimmer	double room

Eine Übernachtung, bitte.
one overnighting, please
One night, please.

Das Zimmer nehme ich/nehmen wir.
the room take I/take we
I/we'll take the room.

Das Zimmer gefällt mir/uns nicht.
the room pleases to-me/to-us not
I/we don't like the room.

Wann gibt es Frühstück?
when gives it breakfast
When is breakfast?

In Germany, breakfast is almost always included in the price. It is the usual "continental breakfast", although in Germany this tends to be larger than elsewhere, with rolls, bread, jam, cheese, sausage, perhaps honey (often from little packets as in airline catering) and, of course, tea or coffee.

Wecken Sie uns bitte morgen früh um sechs (Uhr).
wake you us please tomorrow early at six (clock)
Could you wake us tomorrow morning at six, please.

toilets – die Toiletten

Herren	Men/Gents	**Damen**	Ladies

Wo ist die Toilette?
where is the toilet
Where is the toilet?

Ich muss mal.
I must once
colloquial: I have to go to the toilet.

das Toilettenpapier	toilet paper
die Seife	soap
das Handtuch	towel
die Binde	sanitary towel
der Tampon	tampon

camping – das Camping

Camping is very popular in the German-speaking countries – not only with tents, but also with campers – and there are many excellent camp sites. The local **Fremdenverkehrsamt** ("tourist office") will give you the details.

Wie viel kostet es für ein Zelt (und ein Auto)?
how much costs it for a tent (and a car)
How much is it for a tent (and a car)?

Wo gibt es hier Trinkwasser?
where gives it here drinkwater
Where is there drinking water here?

der Strom	electricity
das Wohnmobil	camper
der Wohnwagen	caravan

Travelling around Germany

nach links	to the left
nach rechts	to the right
geradeaus	straight ahead
die Straße	road, street
der Weg	road, way
die Bundesstraße	federal road *like a British A-road*
die Autobahn	motorway , freeway
weit	far
nah, nicht weit	near

Wie kommt man in die Stadt?
how comes one into the town
Which is the way into town?

Wie weit ist es nach Bremen?
how far is it to Bremen
How far it is to Bremen?

to go

In English we can say "to go" when we mean walking or travelling by car, train, etc. In German you have to use different words:

Ich will in die Stadt gehen.
I want in the town to-go
I want to go/walk into town.

Ich will in die Stadt fahren.
I want in the town to-drive
I want to drive into town.

For both examples, we could simply say:

Ich will in die Stadt.
I want in the town
I want to go into town.

The verb for "to go" is understood without actually being specified. You will hear this construction very often.

... by train

There are several categories of train in Germany. You should be aware of this, since it often affects the fare.

ICE-Sprinter non-stop high speed long distance train. A meal, drinks and a newspaper are included in the fare for 1st class tickets. There is also 2nd class.
ICE (= InterCityExpress) a high speed long distance trains at approx. 170 m/h. 1st and 2nd class
IC, EC (= InterCity, EuroCity) fast trains at approx. 120 m/h. 1st and 2nd class.
Zuschlag surcharge for all the fast trains listed above
D-Zug, IR (= InterRegio) trains, which stop regularly

Nahverkehrszug
local trains, e.g. **RegionalExpress (RE)**, **StadtExpress (SE)**, **RegionalBahn (RB)**.

The German railway system is highly impressive (although the local network less so) and a lot of money is spent on it. Unfortunately, fares tend to be high, unless you can work out one of the rather complicated special offers.

Though the German word for "railways" is strictly speaking **die Eisenbahn**, *people generally just say* **die Bahn**.

der Zug	train
der (Haupt-)Bahnhof	(main) station
der Bahnsteig; das Gleis	platform; platform (track)
die Auskunft	information
die Ankunft	arrival
die Abfahrt	departure
die Fahrkarte	ticket
der Eingang	entrance, way in
der Ausgang	exit, way out
der Fahrkartenschalter	ticket counter
der Fahrkarten-automat	ticket vending machine
die Rückfahrkarte	return ticket
die Platzkarte	reservation
pünktlich	on time, punctual
der Schlafwagen	sleeping car
der Speisewagen	restaurant car
der Fahrplan	timetable
der Anschluss	connection
umsteigen	to change trains
Nichtraucher	non-smokers compartment

Travelling around Germany

The usual word for "to buy" is **kaufen**.

Ich möchte eine Fahrkarte lösen.
I like a ticket buy
I would like to buy a ticket.

Einfach erste/zweite Klasse nach Stuttgart, bitte.
simple 1st/2nd class to Stuttgart, please
A 1st/2nd class single to Stuttgart, please.

Hält dieser Zug in Dortmund?
stops this train in Dortmund
Does this train stop in Dortmund?

Der Zug hat Verspätung.
the train has lateness
The train is late.

... by bus

Travelling by long-distance bus is less common than in Britain or the United States:

der Bus	bus
der Busbahnhof	bus station

... by air

der Flughafen	airport
das Flugzeug	aircraft
der Abflug	departure
die Ankunft	arrival
(die) **Lufthansa**	Germany's national airline

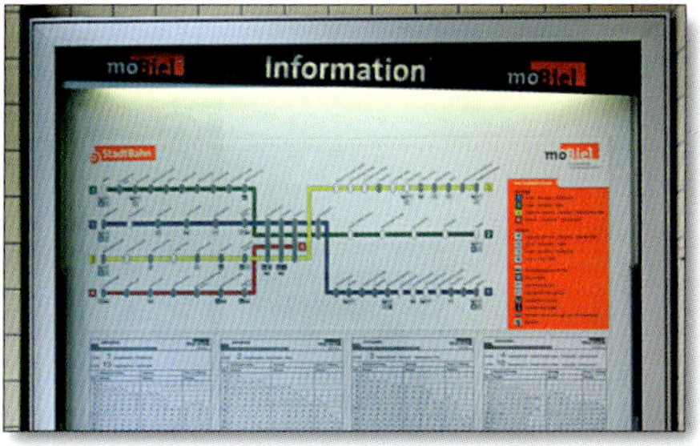

... by boat

You may well like the idea of cruising up the Rhine (**Rhein**) and visiting such places as Cologne (**Köln**), **Koblenz**, **Boppard**, **Bacharach**, **Rüdesheim**, **Bingen**, **Mainz**, etc. Not only are the many castles perched on the rocks along the craggy Rhine valley (**das Rheintal**) highly picturesque, but they also provide a fascinating insight into Germany's history, into former times when the country was composed of hundreds of independent principalities, each trying to extract a toll from travellers.

The German word for "customs", **der Zoll**, *is related to "toll".*

Was kostet die Fahrt?
what costs the journey
How much is the trip?

Wir möchten bis nach Mainz fahren.
we would-like until to Mainz to-drive
We'd like to go (i.e. sail) as far as Mainz.

Wann erreichen wir Koblenz?
when reach we Koblenz
When do we reach Koblenz?

... by car

Germany has a dense network of roads. They tend to be good so, that being said, I'll tell you what to watch out for. They are often poorly lit, especially at the entrances to motorways, so make sure you don't go down the wrong slip road and end up on the wrong side of the motorway (**die Autobahn**): don't be a **Geisterfahrer** (literally: "ghost driver"). Greater use of cats' eyes would improve the lighting no end, but they seem to be used almost only at roadworks.

Apart from where expressly marked there's no speed limit on the **Autobahnen**, and, even though you might be doing a respectable 120 or 130 kilometres an hour, there'll be loads of people bombing past you. There's a lot of expensive and powerful equipment on the German roads and the owners are keen to give you the benefit of it, too. Trying to keep your distance is hopeless, and driving mores are growing more aggressive all the time.

signs

STAU	traffic jam ahead
GLATTEIS	icy road
AUSFAHRT	motorway exit
BEI NÄSSE 80	when wet 80 km/h
LANGSAM FAHREN	drive slowly
EINBAHNSTRAßE	one-way street
UMLEITUNG	diversion
ANWOHNER	"residents"

When the sign **ANWOHNER** *is posted below a parking sign only residents may park there with a special permit. Motorway signs are blue, others yellow.*

das Benzin; der Super	petrol, gasoline; four-star petrol
bleifrei – verbleit	unleaded – leaded
Diesel	diesel oil
das Öl	oil
das Wasser	water
die Luft	air
die Raststätte	service area
die Tankstelle	petrol/gas station
die Panne	breakdown
einen Platten	puncture
reparieren	to repair
der Parkplatz	parking space
die Parkuhr	parking meter
der Führerschein	driving licence
der Unfall	crash, accident
die Autowaschanlage	carwash

Bitte volltanken.
please full-to-tank
Fill her up, please.

Der Wagen springt nicht an.
the car springs not on
The car won't start.

die Batterie	battery
die Bremsen	brakes
die Kupplung	clutch
der Motor	engine
das Getriebe	gears
die Scheinwerfer	lights
die Scheibenwischer	windscreen wipers
die Zündkerzen	spark plugs
der Kühler	radiator
die Reifen	tyres
das Rad	wheel
die Räder	wheels
das Auto, der Wagen	car
das Motorrad	motorbike
ein merkwürdiges Geräusch	a strange noise

hitchhiking – das Trampen

Germany is excellent for hitchhiking. A good place is the motorway service areas – don't go on the motorway itself, of course. A cardboard sign with your destination on it is often a good idea.

Wo fahren Sie hin?
where drive you to
Where are you going?

Setzen Sie mich bitte hier ab.
set you me please here off
Drop me off here, please.

In big cities there is also a **Mitfahrzentrale** (*with-drive-agency*). People who do not want to waiste a full tank of gas on a long trip all alone sign up there, offering to share the ride with others. It is only half the price of a train ticket if not less.

Seeing the sights

Germany is a highly picturesque country. Generally, towns are a lot tidier and cleaner than they are in Britain, although British cities do have a certain buzz in the air which you rarely find in Germany. The exception is Berlin, which has become a cultural centre of Europe, since it is Germany's capital again.

die Sehenswürdigkeiten	sights
der Stadtplan	town plan
die Touristen-information	tourist information
der Park, die Grünanlage	park, green space
das Denkmal	monument
die Burg	castle
das Schloss	castle, palace
der Dom	cathedral
die Kirche	church
der Markt	market
der Marktplatz	marketplace
das Gebäude	building
das Rathaus	town hall
(die) **Fachwerkhäuser**	half-timbered houses
der Brunnen	fountain
die Altstadt	old part of town
die Innenstadt	town centre
der Hafen	harbour, port
der Zoo, der Tiergarten	zoo
die Gasse	narrow street
die Allee	wide alley

Gibt es eine Ermäßigung für Studenten?
gives it a reduction for students
Is there a reduction for students?

Das ist sehr schön.
That is very beautiful/nice.

Bis wann haben Sie auf?
until when have you open
When are you open till?

For "open" you can also say **geöffnet** *or* **offen**; *"closed":* **geschlossen** *or* **zu**.

Ich will einen Stadtbummel machen.
I want a city-walk-around to-make
I'd like to have a look around the town.

The most famous german sights or events are:

der Kölner Dom
the Cologne Dom

Schloss Neuschwanstein
"fairy tale" castle in Bavaria

Rosenmontagszug
the bis shrovetime event in Cologne, Mainz, Düsseldorf (february)

Oktoberfest
beer festival in Munich (october)

Loveparade
raver and techno party in the city of Berlin around the **Brandenburger Tor** (july)

die Reeperbahn
red-light district and nightlife area in Hamburg

die CSD-Parade
= Christopher Street Day. Most important gay event in Germany. The largest is in Cologne (july)
der Christkindlmarkt
the most famous Chrristmas market in Nürnberg

Ich würde gerne ... besichtigen/besuchen/ erleben.
I would like ... to-view/to-visit/to-experience.
I would like to see/visit/take part in the ...

getting around town

By bus (**der Bus**) of course and, in the major cities, also by **U-Bahn** (short for **Untergrund-bahn**, "underground railway"). Many cities still run trams (**S-Bahn**, short for **Straßen-bahn** or **Stadtbahn**) which partially may go underground as well. Travelling without pay-ing might look temptingly easy (**schwarz-fahren** – "*black riding*") - since there are no tik-ket barriers, but if you are "controlled" (**kon-trolliert**) no excuses are accepted and it's out with the readies: generally about 40 – 50 Euros on the spot.

die (Bus-) Haltestelle (bus) stop; also used for trams
die U-Bahnstation underground station

Culture

If your German's weak a lot of what's on offer will pass you by, especially as most foreign films are dubbed into German. Germany has many important cultural centres of world standard – **Berlin**, **Frankfurt**, **Hamburg**, **München**, **Köln**, **Düsseldorf**, **Stuttgart**, etc. – rather than things being centred on one or two cities as in say England.

das Theater	theatre
das Museum	museum
das Kino	cinema
die Ausstellung	exhibition
die Oper	opera
die Messe	(trade)fair
das Konzert	concert
die Galerie	art gallery
die Bibliothek	library
Moderne Kunst	modern art
das Musical	musical
die Eintrittskarte	entrance ticket
ausverkauft	sold out
Pause	break

Was läuft im Kino/im Theater/in der Oper?
what runs in-the cinema/in-the theatre/in the opera
What's playing at the cinema/theatre/opera?

Um wie viel Uhr fängt die Vorstellung an?
at how much clock begins the show on
At what time is the show?

Läuft der Film in OMU oder Originalversion?
runs the film in original-with-subtitles or original-version
Is it with subtitles or not dubbed?

Nightlife – Nachtleben

die Kneipe	pub	**die Bar**	bar
der Club	club	**die Disco**	discothek

As in most European countries young people in Germany likje to go dancing on Friday and Saturday evening. You may have to pass a **Türsteher** (doorman) and have your clothing checked out or even let him bodycheck you. Conveniently there is always a **Garderobe** (cloakroom) where you can even leave your bag. You mostly will not need any cash inside the club, since you will get a **Verzehrkarte** (consumption-card), which has to be paid upon leaving. The entrance fee is charged additionally, unless there is **Mindestverzehr** (least-consumption). One or two drinks are then included in the entrance fee.

Hast Du Lust heute Abend mit in den Club zu kommen?
have you interest today evening with in the club to to-come
Would you like to come to the club with us tonight?

Since clubs are a great place to pick up someone, you may want to be familiar with this vocabulary:

flirten	to flirt	**küssen**	to kiss
bumsen	to fuck	**verliebt**	in love
eifersüchtig	jealous	**das Kondom**	condom
schwul	gay	**lesbisch**	lesbian

Hast du mal Feuer?
have you once fire
Do you have a light?

Bist du alleine hier?
are you alone here
Are you here alone?

Nein, ich bin mit meinem Freund/meiner Freundin hier.
no, I am with my friend/my female-friend here
No. I'm here with my boyfriend/girlfriend.

Was möchtest Du trinken?
what like you to-drink
What would you like to drink?

Gehen wir noch zu dir oder zu mir?
to-go we still to your or to mine
Shall we go to your place or mine?

Sport – Der Sport

If you're a football fan you will know the **Bundesliga**, the German "1st Division". The most popular clubs are **Bayern München** (Munich), the "ManU" of Germany, **Borussia Dortmund**, **Hertha BSC Berlin**, **Bayer 04 Leverkusen**, **VfB Stuttgart**, **Werder Bremen. Schalke 04**, from the industrial city of Gelsenkirchen, is probably about the closest there is to a British-style club.

der Ausflug	excursion
der See	lake
die See, das Meer	sea
der Fluss	river
das Ufer	river bank
der Strand	beach
der Sand	sand
schwimmen	to swim
surfen	to surf
segeln	to sail
das Schwimmbad	swimming pool
angeln gehen	to go angling
die Brücke	bridge
das Feld	field
der Wald	wood, forest
der Baum	tree
das Dorf	village
wandern	to hike
der Berg	mountain

der Schnee	snow
das Fahrrad	bicycle
Ski laufen	to ski
das Fußballspiel	football match

Food & drinks

essen	to eat	**trinken**	to drink
das Messer	knife	**die Gabel**	fork
der Löffel	spoon	**der Teller**	plate
die Tasse	cup	**die Untertasse**	saucer
das Glas	glas	**das Kännchen**	jug, pot

die Mahlzeit	meal
die Speisekarte	menu
das Frühstück	breakfast
das Mittagessen	lunch
das Brunch	runch
das Abendbrot	dinner
die Vorspeise	starter
der Nachtisch	dessert
die Suppe	soup
das Hauptgericht	main course
der Kuchen	cake
die Torte	cream cake
das Teilchen	pastry
das Eis	ice, ice-cream

Germans say **Mahlzeit** *to each other at lunchtime, meaning "enjoy your meal" – there is no real equivalent of this in English.*

Abendbrot: *literally = "evening bread", and in fact this meal tends to be based on bread – like a glorified version of breakfast.*

Ich habe Hunger.
I have hunger
I'm hungry.

Ich habe Durst.
I have thirst
I'm thirsty.

Less frequently heard are **Ich bin hungrig**, *"I am hungry", and* **Ich bin durstig**, *"I am thirsty".*

Food & drinks

Die Speisekarte/die Rechnung, bitte.
the menu/the bill, please
The menu/the bill, please.

Zahlen, bitte.
to-pay, please
The bill, please.

Stimmt so!
agrees so
Keep the change!
The rest is for you! etc.

Hat die Küche noch auf?
has the kitchen still open
Is the kitchen still open?

Depending on where you are, instead of **Brötchen** *you may also hear the terms* **die Semmel, die Schrippe** *and* **der Weck**.

das Brot	bread
das Brötchen	roll
die Butter	butter
das Ei, die Eier	egg(s)
der Aufschnitt	cold cuts
der Käse	cheese
der Schinken	gammon
roher Schinken	ham
der Honig	honey
die Marmelade	jam
der Kaffee	coffee
der Tee	tea
der Zucker	sugar
die Milch	milk
die Sahne	cream
der Süßstoff	sweetener
der Milchkaffee	latte macchiato
der Saft	juice
das Wasser	water

der Kakao	cocoa
das Obst	fruit
der Apfel	apple
die Birne	pear
die Beeren	berries
die Banane	banana
die Apfelsine	orange
die Trauben	grapes
die Pampelmuse	grapefruit
das Gemüse	vegetable
das Fleisch	meat
der Fisch	fish
Meeresfrüchte	seafood
das Geflügel	poultry
das Wild	venison
Lamm	lamb
Kalb	veal
Rind	beef
Schwein	porc
die Wurst	sausage
Ente; Huhn	duck; chicken
die Kartoffeln	potatoes
der Reis	rice
die Möhren	carottes
der Salat	salad, lettuce
die Erbsen	peas
die Bohnen	beans
die Tomaten	tomatoes
der Kohl	cabbage
das Salz	salt
der Pfeffer	pepper
die Gewürze	spices
die Kräuter	herbs

Food & drinks

I don't think I've ever been disappointed in a German restaurant. The food is good, the portions are generous and prices relatively low. There are so many eating places and pubs around you'll find something going on even if German streets can seem quiet.

German towns and cities are now full of Italian, Greek, Turkish, Chinese style restaurants, plus fewer Indian, Vietnamese, Mexican, Korean, etc., as well as the more expensive Japanese or French restaurants. Naturally enough, there are also restaurants where you can enjoy "traditional" German fare based on pork, beef, potatoes, **Sauerkraut,** etc., **gut bürgerlich,** impossible to translate but actually meaning something like "good old grandma's style".

If all else fails – or you're fairly broke – you're bound to find a **Pommes-Bude**, a "chippie" (chips/fries shop) where you'll also be able to buy various types of fried sausage such as **Bratwurst, Currywurst** (sliced fried sausage with curry sauce), **Frankfurter** and **Bockwurst** (a large **Frankfurter**) as well as **Frikadellen** (meat patties). The usual international hamburger chains also have a high profile in German cities.

*Tips and VAT (**MwSt. = Mehrwertsteuer**) are already included in the price. Tipping usually consists of rounding up by a few Euros or so.*

German specialties

Eintopf	stew – often a complete meal
Schlachtplatte	assorted sausage meats
Eisbein	pork knuckle
Sauerbraten	braised beef
Schweineschnitzel	pork cutlet, schnitzel
Wiener Schnitzel	veal in breadcrumbs
Strammer Max	open sandwich with fried egg & ham

Handkäse mit Musik	a nice stinky cheese – you provide the music yourself!
Bismarck Hering	pickled herring
Reibekuchen	potato pancake
Knödel	bread crumb dumpling
Kartoffelsalat	potato salad
Röst-/Bratkartoffeln	fried potatoes
Salzkartoffeln	boiled potatoes
Pommes (frites)	chips/French fries
Sauerkraut	pickled cabbage

Guten Appetit!
good appetite
Enjoy your meal!

Was können Sie heute empfehlen?
what can you today recommend
What do you recommend today?

drinks – Getränke

Germany is famous for its beer, but also its wines and there are enough pubs (**Kneipen**), restaurants (**Gaststätten**) and other **Lokale** around to try them in.

Most German beer is what we call "lager". In German it is correctly called **Pils** and this type of beer is available everywhere in Germany. To order, you can simply say **Bier**, "beer". But depending on the area you may be asked which kind you want. Draft beer is **Bier vom Fass** (= *beer from the barrel*). Other beers are **Alt**

The other side of the Rhine, the **Rheingau**, *is highly picturesque and produces some excellent wines – try to visit* **Schloss Johannisberg** *if you get the chance.*

Take the ferry across the Rhine from **Ingelheim-Freiweinheim** *to* **Oestrich-Winkel**.

Personally I'm not one of the world's great connoisseurs – if I like it, it's good.

(= old), a dark beer which is brewed and served mainly in the area around Düsseldorf, **Weißbier** (= *white beer*) or **Weizenbier** (= *wheat beer*), which are brewed from wheat grain, mainly in Bavaria, **Kölsch** (= Cologne beer), a watery lager, only available in the Cologne area.

Wine in Germany is much cheaper than in Britain, especially, of course, in the southern wine-growing regions of the Rhine valley (**Rheintal**), the Moselle (**Mosel**), **Baden – Württemberg**, and Franconia (**Franken**) in northern Bavaria. Most German wines are white but there are some reds, notably from **Ingelheim am Rhein** (between **Mainz** and **Bingen**), which even calls itself **die Rotweinstadt** (= the red-wine-town).

Einen trockenen/süßen Weißwein/Rotwein, bitte.
A dry/sweet white wine/red wine, please.

Ich hätt' gern 'n Pils.Einen Schnaps, bitte.
I would-have like a pils   a schnaps, please
I'd like a Pils, please.   A Schnaps, please.

Sekt is much cheaper than the French variety, but very palatable. (**Sekt**)

der Sekt	German "Champagne"
die Apfelschorle	apple juice with sparkling water
der Radler/ das Alster	beer with lemonade
der Glühwein	mulled wine *(at Christmas time)*
der Likör	liqueur

Shopping

In Germany there exists a law on closing times (**Ladenschlussgesetz**), which formerly defined shop opening hours to be 9.00 a.m. to 6 - 6.30 p.m. on weekdays, including a closing time around noon and on Wednesday afternoon. On Saturdays until 1.30 - 2.00 p.m. Bakeries were not allowed to sell anything on Sundays. Since the 90's these rules and regulations are constantly changing for the better and opening times have become more flexible. Depending on the area you are staying in, shops may be open until 8.00, 10.00 or 12.00 p.m. on weekdays and Saturdays . But they also may open later or just follow the old regulations. Bakeries may sell their items on Sundays till 11 or 12 a.m.

Gas stations provide the most important items for your household, food, and drinks at extremely high prices, since most of them are open seven days a week and 24hrs.

der Laden, das Geschäft	shop
der Supermarkt	supermarket
die Kaufhalle, das Kaufhaus	department store
der Flohmarkt	flea market
das Lebensmittel-geschäft	grocery store
die Bäckerei	baker's
das Reformhaus	health food shop
die Apotheke	chemist's
der Friseur	hairdresser's
der Optiker	optician's

Wo ist die nächste Buchhandlung?
where is the next bookshop
Where's the nearest bookshop?

Ausverkauf	**Schlussverkauf**
sale	closing-down sale

Würden Sie mir bitte helfen?
would you to-me please help
Could you help me, please?

The little word **Hallo!** *is often used to address a salesperson.*

Wie viel?
how much
How much?

Was kostet das?
what costs that
How much does it cost?

Haben Sie Filme?
have you films
Do you have film?

Nein, haben (verkaufen) wir nicht.
no have (sell) we not
No, we don't.

Ich verstehe nicht, schreiben Sie es bitte auf.
I understand not, write you it please down
I don't understand, would you mind writing it down.

Wo kann ich das anprobieren?
Where can I this try-on
Where can I try this on?

Haben Sie das auch kleiner/größer?
have you this also smaller/larger
Have you got it in a smaller/larger size?

Gefällt es Ihnen?
like it you
Do you like it?

Nein, es ist nicht das Richtige.
no, it is not the right-thing
No, it's not what I am looking for.

das Buch	book
die Zeitung	newspaper
die Zeitschrift	magazine
die Schallplatte	record
die CD	compact disc
die Kassette	cassette
der Stadtplan	town map
die Hose	trousers
das Hemd	shirt
die Bluse	blouse
das T-Shirt	t-shirt
die Jacke	jacket
die Zigaretten	cigarettes
der Rock	skirt
die Schuhe	shoes
die Socken	socks
Taschentuch	tissue
die Unterwäsche	underwear
der Diafilm	slide film
der Schmuck	jewellery
der Hut	hat
das Make-up	make up
die Kleidung	clothes
das Souvenir	souvenir
Lebensmittel	food

Service

post office – die Post

Opening hours vary, depending on the size of the town. But they are definitely open from 9 a.m. - 6 p.m. (Saturdays till 12 noon). Letter boxes can easily be recognized, since they are yellow. Sometimes there are still two, one for local letters, the other for all other destinations.

die Briefmarke	stamp
der Brief	letter
das Fax	fax
das Telegramm	wire
das Päckchen	small parcel
das Paket	parcel
die Eilzustellung	express delivery
per Einschreiben	registered letter, certified letter
die Ansichtskarte	picture postcard
die Postkarte	postcard

telecommunications – die Telekommunikation

You can make international calls from all telephone boxes in Germany, mostly operated by the **Deutsche Telekom**. The majority can only be operated by phonecard (**Telefonkarte**) which is available at tobacco shops, railroad stations, at a kiosk and of course in the official shop of the Deutsche Telekom (**T-Punkt**). Only few telephone boxes can be operated with coins or with a credit card. Your cell phone will probably work, depending on the international roaming contracts between your provider and the german telephone companies.

You can send a fax (**das Fax**) at post-offices, department stores, railway stations, the airport, etc. using a fax box – very similar to telephone boxes. These generally can only be operated by telephone card.

If you are looking for an **Internetcafé** *you may want to know, that all the internet and e-mail vocabulary is basically English.*

die Telefonzelle	telephone box
die Vermittlung	operator
das R-Gespräch	reverse-charge/ collect call
die Vorwahl-Nummer, die Ortskennzahl	area code
das Ferngespräch	long-distance call

banks – die Banken

You can cash money with your credit card or Eurocheque card at a cash machine (**der Geldautomat**) outside of any bank, in airports, railway stations, gas stations and even department stores. If you need to cash traveller cheques you are dependent on the bank opening hours from 8.30 a.m.–1.30 p.m. and 2.30 p.m.–4.00 or 5.00 p.m. on weekdays. Or you can exchange the traveller cheques at large railway stations and airports.

Ich möchte Geld wechseln.
I like money to-change
I would like to change money.

die Kreditkarte	credit card
das Pfund	pound (sterling)
der Dollar	dollar
der Euro	euro

At the doctor's – Beim Arzt

You should have some health insurance policy before travelling. However, German medicine is high-tech and super-efficient. The number to ring in an emergency in Germany is 112 (Police: 110). All important Emergency numbers are marked clearly in telephone boxes and telephone directories.

Ich fühle mich schlecht.
I feel me bad
I don't feel well.

Ich bin krank.
I am ill/sick
I'm ill.

Ich brauche dringend einen Arzt.
I need urgent a doctor
I need a doctor urgently.

Haben Sie Schmerzen?
have you pains
Are you in pain?

Hier tut es weh.
here does it hurt
It hurts here.

Ich habe gebrochen.
I have broken/vomited
I've been sick.

Ich bin schwanger.
I am pregnant.

Ich bin Diabetiker.
I am diabetic.

at the dentist's – beim Zahnarzt

Ich habe Zahnschmerzen.
I have toothpains
I have toothache.

Bitte plombieren, nicht ziehen.
please fill, not pull
Please give me a filling, don't pull the tooth out.

Benutzen Sie bitte ein Betäubungsmittel.
use you please an anaesthetic
Please use an anaesthetic.

at the chemist's – in der Apotheke

das Rezept	prescription
verschreiben	to prescribe
das Arzneimittel	medicine, drug
der Durchfall	diarrhoea
die Verstopfung	constipation
die Magenschmerzen	stomach pains
die Kopfschmerzen	headache
einnehmen	to take

Bitte nehmen Sie die Tabletten vor jeder Mahlzeit ein.
please take you the tablets before every mealtime in
Please take the tablets before each meal.

... nach jeder Mahlzeit. *... after each/every meal*

... dreimal täglich. *... three times a day*

Zur äußerlichen Anwendung.
to-the external use
For external use.

The following important item can be purchased not only at a chemist, but also in supermarkets, gas stations, public laries or drugstores:

Condom, in German **das Kondom**, can also be called **der Pariser** = "frenchman" or **Präser** (short for **Präservativ**, which may have similarities to preservative, but has nothing to do with preserving food).

At the doctor's – Beim Arzt

Parts of the body – Körperteile

der Kopf	head
der Magen	stomach
das Auge	eye
der Bauch	belly, abdomen
das Ohr	ear
das Bein	leg
der Mund	mouth
der Fuß	foot
der Hals	throat, neck
das Herz	heart
der Nacken	(back of) neck
die Lunge	lung
die Hand	hand
die Leber	liver
der Arm	arm
die Nieren	kidneys
die Schulter	shoulder
der Knochen	bone
der Finger	finger
das Fieber	temperature
die Rippe	rib
die Brust	chest, breast
der Rücken	back
die Blase	bladder
die Drüse	gland
das Blut	blood
der Muskel	muscle
der Urin	urine
die Mandeln	tonsils
die Haut	skin

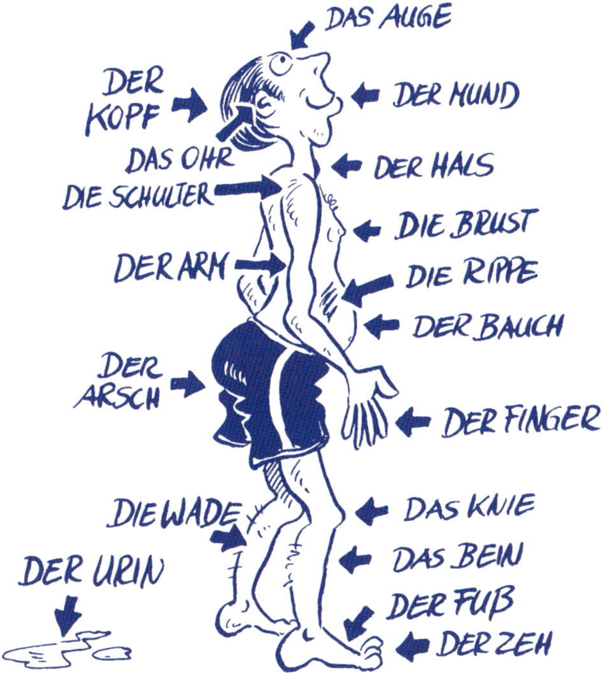
DAS AUGE
DER KOPF
DER MUND
DAS OHR
DER HALS
DIE SCHULTER
DIE BRUST
DER ARM
DIE RIPPE
DER BAUCH
DER ARSCH
DER FINGER
DIE WADE
DAS KNIE
DER URIN
DAS BEIN
DER FUß
DER ZEH

Colloquial words & expressions

It is desperately hard to master colloquial idiom in a foreign language, and I'd advise you to use such phrases sparingly, certainly until your general grasp of the language has "caught up".

Every language has words and phrases which even a professor versed in the obscurest of grammatical niceties won't have a chance of knowing unless he has been to the country and actually spent time with its people. A book like this can give you a few expressions, **schwarz auf weiß** ("*black on white*"), but simply reading them is a poor substitute for hearing them actually used by the natives in the appropriate context.

There are two main areas I want to talk about here. First, the way we often shorten words. Think of "ain't" for "have not". The contraction "haven't" would be immediately recognizable, but "ain't" wouldn't be. Similarly "dunno" for "don't know" and "gonna" for "going to". In German there are also such contractions, especially in conjunction with **du**, the familiar, singular form for "you":

haste = hast du "have you?", Do you have?

Example:
Haste 'n Moment Zeit? =
Hast du einen Moment Zeit?

"Have you a moment time?"
Do you have a moment?

Further examples:

biste = bist du	"are you"
kannste = kannst du	"can you"
willste = willst du	"want you", i.e. Do you want to?

Also note that **wir**, "we", is often pronounced like "mir", especially in Southern Germany. The verb **haben**, "to have", is also frequently contracted to a sound resembling "haam". So you can often hear the following:

mir haam = wir haben we have

You should also know that, in the North, people often say "wat" instead of **was** and "dat" for **das** – like in Dutch. And, in the South, you can hear "des" instead of **das**. In Bavaria you will hear **hashte** for "haste"; in Berlin "g" is pronounced as a "y" (German **j**) – **jehn waa** = **gehen wir**. Almost everywhere you will hear "nee" for **nein** ("no"). Another specialty is a little word tacked onto the end of sentences, expressing a rhetorical question and meaning "right?", "don't you think?", e.g. **gell(e)** in the South, **ne** in southern North-Rhine-Westphalia and **nu** in many regions in East Germany.

As in Britain the difference in accents between North and South is considerable, and there's no way I can even pretend to do justice to the subject.

Er hat wohl recht, gell?	**Toll, ne?**
he has well right, true (etc.)	*great, true (etc.)*
He's probably right, don't you think?	Great, huh?

Colloquial words & expressions

I also want to mention some colloquial phrases which you may well meet. Occasionally, vogue words are on everyone's lips for a while before disappearing. But a lot of colloquial and slang expressions do of course remain common currency for years, and a knowledge of them is often essential to understanding an everyday conversation.

die Schnauze, die Klappe	mouth
Halt die Klappe!	*"hold your mouth"* = Shut up!
Na und?	Who cares? So what?
Prima! Sauber!	Excellent! Super!
Spitze! spitzenmäßig	very much as above, but **geil** can also mean "horny", "randy" (**heiß**)
abhauen – Hau ab!	to piss off, but can also be used humorously
Ich muss mal!	I've got to go (to the loo)!
Hast du's gerafft/ kapiert?	Got it? Understand?
die Knete, die Kohle	money, lolly, spondoolicks
die Bullen	police, the fuzz, pigs
die Kippe/Fluppe	cigarette, fag
Mahlzeit!	said at lunchtime, but also ironically if someone vomits or burps
fressen	"to eat" for animals, but also used for people pigging out

By the way, there is a street in Frankfurt called the **Freßgasse**.

pennen	to sleep, kip
der Penner	dosser, vagrant – can also mean "idiot", "wanker", etc.
die Klamotten	old clothes, togs, but can also mean personal possessions, including furniture, etc.
die Glotze, der Flimmerkasten	TV, gogglebox
Das ist doch 'n Klacks!	It's a doddle/piece of piss! (i.e. very easy)
einen ausgeben	to buy someone a drink
Ich gebe aus.	I'm buying. / I'll treat you.
eine Runde bezahlen	to buy a round (less common in Germany – you normally pay for your own drink)

Getting deeper into it, you'll discover the funny and casual sides of the German language. If you'd like to learn more: get your copy of **German Slang** *Kauderwelsch volume 188. ISBN 978-3-89416-476-8. Available at any book shop throughout Germany, Austria, Switzerland, Belgium, and the Netherlands.*

hartes Zeug	hard stuff
besoffen, blau	drunk, pissed
Das ist jot-wee-dee!	It's miles from nowhere!
wahnsinnig! irrsinnig!	Amazing! Incredible!
Wahnsinn! Irrsinn!	Fantastic!, etc.
Zur Hölle damit!	To hell with it!
Scheiß der Hund drauf!	"*shit the dog on-it*" = I don't give a shit!
jemanden abschleppen	to pick someone up
Scher' dich zum Teufel!	Go to hell!
Lass mich in Ruhe/Frieden!	Leave me alone! *(in silence/peace)*
unheimlich viel/ gut	a great many/ extremely good
ganz heiß sein auf ...	to be keen to... *(= to be hot for)*
hinter dem Mond	= behind the moon (for something or someone backward)

German does, of course, also have its share of slightly less polite terminology. Much of this is based on the word **Scheiße**, "shit", etc., which can also be joined to the following word, eg. **Scheißwetter**, "shit weather", "bloody awful weather". This can also be done with the word **Sau**, "sow", "pig" – **Sauwetter**, slightly less strong in meaning than **Scheißwetter**,

saulangweilig, "horribly (bloody) boring", **saubillig**, "ridiculously cheap" (**spottbillig** is an entirely polite way of expressing the same thing). **Schitt**, slightly less strong in meaning than **Scheiße**, is frequently heard in the North.

I don't aim to give an exhaustive list of such expressions since this isn't a dictionary of slang, but here are a few items for you:

Null/kein Bock!
I couldn't give a damn! I don't want to!
Motz mich nicht an!
Get off my back!
Halt die Klappe/Schnauze!
Shut up!
die Schnauze voll haben
to be fed up/pissed off with something
Sauerei! Schweinerei!
Disgusting! What a disgrace!
jemanden verarschen
to take the piss out of someone;
to mess someone about
Das ist total beschissen!
What a balls-up! It's a complete mess!
So ein Mist!
What a thing to happen! Dammit! Sod it!
der Arschkriecher
arselicker, creep
Leck mich am Arsch!
Kiss my arse! Fuck you!
Er kann/du kannst mich mal!
Even *Goethe*, Germany's national bard, alludes to this expression, so if it's okay for him ...

The political situation in Germany

There are two big differences from the British political situation. To start with, instead of our "first-past-the-post", winner-takes-all system, the Germans have proportional representation – a **Verhältniswahlsystem**. This means that the number of votes cast for a party are actually reflected in the number of seats that the party wins – unless it receives under 5 % of the vote, the so-called "5% hurdle", the **Fünf-Prozent-Hürde**. This is designed to keep out small, fringe parties.

What these arrangements have amounted to in recent years is permanent coalition government, since no one party seems able to win an absolute majority. The largest political parties in alphabetical order are the two **Unionsparteien** – the **Christlich-Demokratische Union** (**CDU**) and the **Christlich-Soziale Union** (**CSU**), the latter operating only in Bavaria, the **Freie Demokratische Partei** (**FDP**), the Greens who have been operating together with a small party – **die Grünen und Bündnis 90**, **Die Linke** and the **Sozialdemokratische Partei Deutschlands** (**SPD**).

The second major difference from the UK is, as Germany's official name the Federal Republic of Germany (**Bundesrepublik Deutschland**, **BRD**) implies, that it is organized on a federal basis. Since the reunification there are sixteeen

Länder (singular: **das Land**), "states", three of them cities: **Bremen**, **Hamburg** and **Berlin**. The other **Länder** are **Flächenländer**, "area states", i.e. states covering actual regions such as **Bayern** (Bavaria), **Hessen** (Hessen), **Niedersachsen** (Lower Saxony), **Baden-Württem-berg**, **Saarland**, **Mecklenburg-Vorpommern** (Mecklenburg-West Pomerania), also called **Meck Pom**, **Sachsen** (Saxony), **Sachsen-Anhalt** (Saxony-Anhalt), **Thüringen** (Thuringia), **Schleswig-Holstein**, **Rheinland-Pfalz** (Rhineland-Palatinate), **Brandenburg** or the most populous state, **Nordrhein-Westfalen** (**NRW**) (North-Rhine-Westphalia).

There are two chambers of government, the **Bundestag**, comparable to our House of Commons, and the **Bundesrat**, where the representatives of the **Länder** governments meet. This system will be more familiar to American than British readers.

The old and new capital (**Hauptstadt**) of Germany is Berlin, after a lengthy period (1948-1990) with Bonn as the capital of the Federal Republic of Germany.

The political situation in Germany

wählen	to vote; to choose, select
der Wähler, die Wählerin	voter (m/f)
die Stimme	vote; voice
der Politiker, die Politikerin	politician (m/f)
der/die Abgeordnete	MP
der Wahlkreis	constituency
das Mandat	seat; mandate
der Bundeskanzler	the Federal Chancellor
der Außenminister	Foreign Minister
die Opposition	opposition
die Koalition	coalition
die Wende	change of government
das Gleichgewicht der Kräfte	balance of power
die Verhandlungen	negotiations
die Verfassung	constitution
das Grundgesetz	Basic Law (*Germany's constitution*)
die Hauptstadt	capital (city)
die Umwelt-verschmutzung	environmental pollution
die Kernenergie	nuclear power
das Atomkraftwerk (AKW)	atomic/nuclear power station
die Arbeitslosigkeit	unemployment

The German economy

Apart from the old eastern german region, Germany is one of the most prosperous societies in the world. You become aware of this as soon as you cross the border or enter the airport terminal. However, re-unification has brought changes. The **Nord-Süd-Gefälle** (North-South divide) within the old West Germany has been superseded by the still clearly marked economic border between East and West. Here is some vocabulary that could be heard during the past years until now in german politics:

die Wirtschaft	economy (also "pub")
die Industrie	industry
die Landwirtschaft	agriculture
der Handel	trade
das Geschäft	business, shop

die Wohlstandsgesellschaft
the affluent society

die Leistungsgesellschaft
achievement-oriented society

die Ellenbogengesellschaft
"elbow society", i.e. rat race

die Steuerlüge
tax lie – The breaching of former chancellor Helmut Kohl's promise, that tax increases would not be necessary for the recovery of East Germany after reunification.

die Währung	currency
der Mauerfall	the fall of the Berlin wall
das Geld	money
die Inflation	inflation
arbeiten; **schaffen**; **malochen**	to work; to graft; etc.

die Arbeitslosigkeit bekämpfen	to combat unemployment
Bergwerke dichtmachen	to close down pits/mines
Massenentlassungen	mass layoffs
Arbeitslosengeld erhalten, **stempeln müssen**	to be on the dole
das Ballungsgebiet	conurbation
das Ruhrgebiet	the Ruhr industrial area
Großraum Frankfurt	Greater Frankfurt
das Rhein-Main-Gebiet	the Rhine-Main conurbation

Volksdeutsche

This is a topic which you may well find coming up on your travels, especially in conversation with older Germans. If you look up **Volksdeutsche(r)** in the dictionary you'll find "ethnic German", but it tends to be used in connection with those Germans still living in regions now belonging to such countries as the Russia, Poland and Romania.

Germany's borders have always been fluid, especially in the East, and German settlement and colonization of such regions began centuries before the Nazis' drive for **Lebensraum**, "living space". During and after the Second World War most of the Germans left or were driven out. Pockets of them, however, still remain in places as far afield as Kazakhstan in Central Asia, others rather nearer "home" in **Siebenbürgen** (Transylvania), or scattered throughout Silesia, formerly German **Schlesien**, now Polish **Šlask.** Many of these **Volksdeutsche** have been returning to Germany for years. The **Aussiedler** (resettlers) are not always easy to integrate. After all, many don't even speak German, their families having adopted, say, Russian, in the course of assimilation into the host communities.

However, others have actively kept up their German traditions. In the summer of 1985, in the market at Tashkent, Uzbekhistan (Central

Volksdeutsche

Over the past few years the political situation in eastern Europe and vast tracts of Asia has been turned on its head. Now, it's no longer a case of those with German ancestry not being allowed out – these days the Federal Republic doesn't really want to allow them in. The rigmarole would-be immigrants have to undergo has been made so involved it takes about two years for their application forms to be processed.

Asia), I was conducting a conversation in German with a member of my travel group. An old lady overheard us and told us she was German and lived with her family in a small village about thirty kilometres away. She spoke not **Hochdeutsch** (High or Standard German) but the old **Schwäbisch** (Swabian) dialect their ancestors had brought from the **Heimat** (homeland) two centuries ago. Obviously, a country's geography will be crucial to its history, and it's interesting to compare Germany and Britain in this respect. Britain's borders are geographical as much as political (perhaps except for in Ireland). For Germany this has never been so, and is a major reason why Britain and Germany have such different histories. A lot of West Germans, or their parents, are from the East. Many of these expellees, the **Heimatvertriebene** ("those driven from their homeland") would still like to see a return of these "homelands", and reminisce about childhood in Breslau (now **Wrocław**), Posen **(Poznań)** or Lemberg **(Lvov).**

die Auswanderung	emigration
die Einwanderung	immigration
die Flucht	flight, escape
flüchten	to flee
der Flüchtling	refugee
die Grenze	border, frontier
die Geschichte	history, story
die Heimat	homeland, home country

die Kolonisation	colonization
die Besiedlung	settlement
die Anlaufstelle	transit camp
germanische/ slawische Stämme	Germanic/ Slavic tribes
Rußland	Russia
Polen	Poland
Ungarn	Hungary
Rumänien	Romania

Guest-workers & foreigners

There are around 7 million foreigners living in Germany. These foreign communities are much in evidence in the towns and cities with their restaurants, shops, etc.. Earlier waves of immigrant **Gastarbeiter** (guest-workers) from southern and eastern Europe are more or less **angepasst** (integrated), but in recent years a new wave has started – especially from countries such as Poland, former Yugoslavia and Romania (i.e. other than the **Volksdeutsche**). In addition, many **Flüchtlinge** (refugees) from the world's crisis regions are seeking **politisches Asyl** (political asylum).

The largest immigrant group in Germany is formed by the Turks and Kurds. As with Pakistanis in Britain or Algerians in France, they have tended to be the butt of racist abuse in Germany. They were originally brought in to do the kind of menial jobs many Germans didn't want to do, but of course at times of high unemployment their position is less secure. Many arrived with the intention of earning good money and then going back home, but ended up staying after all. For some years now, the amount of german money remitted back to Turkey has been declining. The children of these immigrants speak fluent German, go to German schools, have German friends and regard Turkey as a foreign country. The old East Germany also had its guest-workers. These were from Third World states such as Vietnam and Mozambique, as well as neighbouring Poland.

der Gastarbeiter	guest-worker
der Ausländer	foreigner
die Türkei	Turkey
Griechenland	Greece
Italien	Italy
Spanien	Spain
Serbien	Serbia
Kroatien	Croatia
Bosnien	Bosnia
die (Kosovo-) Albaner	(Kosovo-) Albanian
die Kurden	Kurds
Anatolien	Anatolia
der Ausländerhass	"forerigner hatred", xenophobia
das Vorurteil	prejudice
Ausländer raus!	"foreigners out!" (racist slogan)
rechtsradikal	extreme right

The Nazi legacy

On a British stage, a comedian can always get a laugh by appearing in an SS uniform. This would elicit strong reactions in other countries as well, if not exactly laughter. Although the War ended nearly half a century ago and Germany appears to have changed beyond recognition, it will still take generations for those events to be forgotten – if that is the right word. I was in Germany in 1978 – 79, when "Holocaust" was shown on television. In a matter of weeks the entire population – or those who wanted to know – became aware of how much of the country's recent history had been suppressed. Fathers found themselves having to account for their whereabouts during those times to sons and daughters. Skeletons began clanking in cupboards. Since then, however, the Germans, or certainly the German media, cannot be accused of avoiding these issues.

The process of **Vergangenheitsbewältigung** *("getting over / coping with the past") has now been in progress in West Germany for quite a long time. In Austria it started in connection with the election of the ex-Nazi and ex-UN Secretary General Dr. Kurt Waldheim as the country's President in 1986.*

der Nationalsozialismus
National Socialism
der Anschluss
incorporation of Austria into Nazi Germany
die Ostmark
old Nazi name for Austria
der Lebensraum
living space, Lebensraum

der Einfall	invasion
die Endlösung	final solution
die Vernichtung	extermination, annihilation
das Konzentrationslager (KZ)	concentration camp
die Juden	the Jews
die Kriegsverbrechen	war crimes
der Richter	judge
das geteilte Deutschland	divided Germany
die Besatzungsmächte	the occupying powers
die Wiedergutmachung	atonement; reparations
die Ostpolitik	"Ostpolitik" ("East policy") – dialogue with Eastern Europe started by Willy Brandt

The former East German government regarded itself as an antifascist state which had carried out a far more thorough **Entnazifizierung** (denazification) than took place in West Germany. Indeed, much of its propaganda during the '50s and '60s, according to which many old Nazis remained in the West German judiciary, teaching profession and administrative posts was unfortunately true.

However, the current problem of **Rassismus** (racism) and **Fremdenhass** (xenophobia) in the former GDR indicates that the old leadership there had nothing to be smug about. Since unification, a Mozambican has been dragged from a Leipzig tram and kicked to death by skinheads (**Kahlköpfe**); the day the new German-Polish Treaty came into force abolishing the visa requirement between the two countries, hooded young men chanting **Deutschland den Deutschen** (Germany for the Germans) waited at the **Oder-Neiße** border to kick and spit at Polish coaches.

At **Hoyerswerda**, a small town near **Dresden**, the authorities were unable to guarantee the safety of asylum seekers. Although only a small core of fanatics were responsible for the actual violence that occurred, they seem to have had at least the tacit backing of much of the town. In a dramatic climbdown, the authorities bussed the asylum-seekers to the west, where the racism problem is adjudged to be less acute.

But the incident which really shocked the nation's conscience – the horrible disfigurement of a little Lebanese girl when an asylum centre was firebombed – happened in the west. At last, "public opinion" woke up and marginalised the idiots. Late in the day, centre-right politicians realised that playing the race card for electoral gain was literally playing with fire. Only a very few want to travel down that road again.

Unification & old East Germany

1989 was a "Year of Revolutions" in the old **Ostblock** (Eastern bloc). German **Wiedervereinigung** (reunification), which for so long looked an impossibility and took everyone by surprise, actually came about with incredible speed once it started – although what it really amounts to is absorption of the old GDR by the existing Federal Republic.

The **Deutsche Demokratische Republik**, or **DDR** (German Democratic Republic – GDR) was created out of the Soviet occupation zone in 1949 in response to the founding of the **Bundesrepublik Deutschland**, **BRD** (Federal Republic of Germany, FRG) out of the US, British and French zones.

In 1989, what former GDR leader **Erich Honecker** intended to be a splendid 40-year anniversary turned into a personal disaster as the old **Arbeiter- und Bauernstaat** (Workers' and Peasants' State) was swept away by popular discontent. It had been clear for some time that big changes were happening all over eastern Europe, especially after the Hungarians threw open their border with Austria, but even then no one could have expected the avalanche that came.

The scenes as the Berlin Wall (**die Berliner Mauer**) came tumbling down were emotional and moving. "The Germans", Walter Momper, then Mayor of West Berlin announced, "are the happiest people in the world". Historic – and already history. Even though those heady November and December days will never be forgotten, the mood didn't take long to change to one of gloom and even despair. The eastern economy crumbled fast and unemployment rocketed. The former solidarity between **Wessies** (Westerners) and **Ossies** (Easterners) has evaporated. Within the first ten years after re-unification the Ossies complained about being treated like second-class citizens. The euphoria of having Deutschmarks in their pockets, being able to walk into former West Berlin or take a coach trip to Paris or Amsterdam has worn off as the cost of living soars and the old securities of life unraveled.

The former east german **Staatssicherheitsdienst**, better known as the **Stasi** (state security service) also left a depressing legacy: it probed into all aspects of life in East Germany and now that many – although not all – of the files are publicly accessible, people are discovering that neighbours, trusted friends and even spouses were regularly reporting on them to the police.

The Eastern part of Germany will retain its own identity – and remain crisis-ridden – still for years to come. **Sanierung** (economic restructuring) will be long and painful, as well as fabulously expensive. The old East Germany was not without a certain charm, largely because much of the heritage of former ages has

Some of the Wall is being preserved as a memorial: after all, a lot of people were shot trying to cross it.

been preserved (even if more by accident than design).By way of actual sights, in "East" Berlin there is the elegant avenue called **Unter den Linden**, which leads to the **Brandenburger Tor** *(Brandenburg Gate)* where **die Mauer** *(the Wall)* used to run. There is also **Alexanderplatz** *(Alexander Square)* with the **Fernsehturm** *(TV Tower)*, the magnificent **Museumsinsel** ("museum island"), the palace of **Sanssouci** in **Potsdam** (just out-side Berlin), and the suburb of **Köpenick**. Berlin is again growing to be one of the most attractive cities in Germany, as well as the most vibrant and cosmopolitan – a real **Weltstadt** *("world city")*.

The most scenic part in the eastern part of Germany is without doubt **Thüringen** (Thuringia) in the southwest, with its hills, forests and picturesque towns (**Erfurt**, **Weimar**, **Gotha**) and villages. Visit also the **Wartburg** (near **Eisenach**), a tower with a magnificent view of the surrounding hills; here, **Martin Luther** translated the Bible into German and laid the basis of the modern language. The south-east has **Dresden** – with its classical architecture and setting on the river **Elbe** one of the most imposing cities in Germany; nearby **Bautzen** is interesting as the centre of **Sorbisch** (Sorbian) culture (the Sorbian dialects are closely related to Polish and Czech). Around **Berlin** you will find the picturesque lakes and woodlands of **Brandenburg**, and along the northern coast **Wismar**, **Rostock**, **Stralsund** as well as the delightful island of **Rügen** are all worth a visit (from the latter there's also a ferry to Denmark).

sound)))trip®
New at
Reise Know-How
Reise Know-How
Iceland
978-3-8317-5114-3
The Andes
978-3-8317-5111-2
Scotland
978-3-8317-5118-1
Turkey
978-3-8317-5120-4
Ireland
978-3-8317-5117-4
Bellydance
978-3-8317-5113-6
Cuba
978-3-8317-5105-1
Switzerland
978-3-8317-5104-4
Northeast Brazil
978-3-8317-5107-5
The Balkans
978-3-8317-5103-7
The sound)))trip compilations introduce typical & up-to-date music of a country or region.
With this series of audio CDs we are trying to give music fans & travellers a musical insight into different regions of the world.
As a warm-up before travelling, as a lasting memory thereafter, or purely as an audio discovery trip, allow yourself to be surprised by the musical diversity of our world.
Audio-CD,
50–60 minutes duration,
22-sided booklet.
Recommended price:
15,90 € [D]
in cooperation with:
(((piranha)))
MP3 audio sample on the Internet:
www.reise-know-how.de

Vocabulary English – German

A

abandon, to verlassen
able to, to be können
about etwa; über
accident Unfall, der; Unglück, das
achieve, to erreichen
address Adresse, die; Anschrift, die
admittedly freilich
affair Sache, die
after nach
after all doch
afterwards dann
air Luft, die
aircraft Flugzeug, das
airmail Luftpost, die
airport Flughafen, der
alight aussteigen
all alles
allow, to erlauben
allowed, to be dürfen
alone allein
already schon
also auch
always immer
anaesthetic Betäubungsmittel, das
and und
angling, to go angeln gehen
angry sauer; wütend
animal Tier, das
answer, to antworten
any jede, -r, -s
appear, to scheinen
appetite Appetit, der
apple Apfel, der
approximately etwa
arm Arm, der
A-road (Br.) Bundesstraße, die
arrival Ankunft, die
arrive, to ankommen
as als
as … as so … wie
assume, to vermuten
at an, bei
at home zu Hause
at lunchtime mittags
at night nachts
at once gleich
at that time damals
aunt Tante, die

B

bad schlecht
bad luck das Pech
baker Bäcker, der
bakery Bäckerei, die
ball Ball, der
bank Bank, die
bath Bad, das
bathe, to baden
bathroom Badezimmer, das
be, to sein
beach Strand, der
be meant, to sollen
beautiful schön
because weil
become, to werden
bed Bett das

beer Bier, das
before bevor, vor
begin, to beginnen
beginning Beginn, der
bench (Sitz-)Bank, die
Berlin Wall Berliner Mauer, die
best, the beste, der/die/das
better besser
bicycle (Fahr-)Rad, das
big groß
bitter bitter
black schwarz
Bless you! (after sneezing) Gesundheit!
bloke Typ, der
blood Blut, das
blue blau
book Buch, das
border Grenze, die
both beide
bottle Flasche, die
boy Junge, der
boyfriend Freund, der
brake Bremse, die
bread Brot, das
bread roll Brötchen, das
break, to brechen
breakdown (car) Panne, die
breakfast Frühstück, das
breast Brust, die
bridge Brücke, die
broken kaputt
brother Bruder, der
brother-in-law Schwager, der
brown braun
building Gebäude, das
bus Bus, der
bus station Busbahnhof, der
bus stop Bushaltestelle, die
business Geschäft, das
busy besetzt, beschäftigt
but aber; sondern
butter Butter, die
buy, to kaufen
by von
Bye! Tschüss! Tschüs!

C

cake Kuchen, der; Torte, die
called, to be heißen
camp Lager, das
camping Camping, das
camping site Campingplatz, der
can (he/she) kann (er/sie)
car Auto, das; Wagen, der
carry, to tragen
case Sache, die
cassette Kassette, die
cast, to (metal) gießen
castle Schloss, das
cat Katze, die
cause Ursache, die
certain sicher
certified letter Einschreiben, das
champagne Champagner, der
change, to (money) wechseln
change, to (train) umsteigen
cheap billig
cheap hotel Pension, die
cheerful munter
chest Brust, die
chicken Huhn, das
child Kind, das
children Kinder, die
chips; fries Pommes frites, die
chocolate Schokolade, die
choose, to wählen
Christmas Weihnachten
cigarette Zigarette, die
cinema Kino, das
city Stadt, die
clean sauber
cleanliness

Sauberkeit, die
climb in, to einsteigen
clock Uhr, die
close, to schließen
closed geschlossen; zu
clothes Kleidung; die
cloud Wolke, die
coach Bus, der
coach station Busbahnhof, der
coffee Kaffee, der
cold kalt
comb Kamm, der
Come on! Los!
come, to kommen
compare, to vergleichen
compartment Abteil, das
concert Konzert, das
connection Anschluss, der; Verbindung, die
conversation Gespräch, das
core Kern, der
corner Ecke, die
correct richtig
cost, to kosten
count, to zählen
country Land, das
couple Paar, das
course Gang, der
court (of law) Gericht, das
crazy verrückt
cream Sahne, die
cup Tasse, die

D

daily täglich
dance Tanz, der
dance, to tanzen
data Daten, die
date Datum, das
day Tag, der
dead tot
dear teuer
death Tod, der
declare, to erklären
delay Verspätung, die
delicious lecker
departure Abfahrt, die; Abflug, der
desire Lust, die
dictionary Wörterbuch, das
difficult schwierig; schwer
dining car Speisewagen,der
disaster Unglück, das
dish Gericht, das
diversion Umleitung, die
do you like it? gefällt es dir/Ihnen?
doctor Arzt, der
dog Hund, der
door Tür, die
draw, to ziehen
dress (for ladies) Kleid, das
drinking water Trinkwasser, das
drive, to fahren
driving licence Führerschein,der
drug Arzneimittel,das
drunk (colloq.) blau
dry trocken
during the day tagsüber
duty Pflicht, die

E

each jede, -s
ear Ohr, das
early früh
earth Erde, die
East Osten, der
Easter Ostern
eastern östlich
eat, to essen
economy Wirtschaft, die
egg Ei, das
either ... or entweder ... oder
end Ende, das
end, to beenden

English Englisch, englisch
Enjoy your meal! Guten Appetit!
enough genug
entrance Eingang, der
error Irrtum, der
escape, to entkommen
evening Abend, der
evening, in the abends
every jede, -r, -s
everything alles
example Beispiel, das
excursion Ausflug, der
exit Ausgang, der
expensive teuer
explain, to erklären
express delivery Eilzustellung,die
express, to ausdrücken
eye Auge, das

F

false falsch
far weit
farmer Bauer, der
fast schnell
father Vater, der
feet Füße, die
ferry Fähre, die
fever Fieber, das
field Feld, das
fill in/out, to ausfüllen
fill, to (teeth) plombieren
find, to finden
finger Finger, der
finish, to beenden
finished fertig
fire Feuer, das
first erste(r)
fish Fisch, der
fishing, to go angeln gehen
floor Etage, die; Stockwerk, das
fly, to fliegen
follow, to folgen
food Lebensmittel, die
food shop Lebensmittelgeschäft, das
foot Fuß, der
football Fußball, der
for für
for example (e.g.) zum Beispiel (z.B.)
foreign currency exchange office Wechselstube, die
foreigner Ausländer(in), der (die)
forest Wald, der
fork Gabel, die
form Formular, das
France Frankreich
free frei
freedom Freiheit, die
freeway Autobahn, die
French Französisch, französisch
friend Freund(in), der (die)
friendly freundlich
from aus, von
frontier Grenze, die
frost Frost, der
fruit Obst, das

G

game Spiel, das
gas station Tankstelle, die
gasoline Benzin, das
German Deutsch, deutsch
German champagne Sekt, der
get going Los!
get in, to einsteigen
get out, to aussteigen
get, to bekommen
get to know, to kennenlernen
gift Geschenk, das
girl Mädchen, das
girlfriend Freundin, die
give, to geben; schenken
glasses Brille, die

go for a walk, to spazieren gehen
go, to fahren; gehen
God Gott, der
gone (he's) gegangen (er ist ?)
good gut
Good evening! Guten Abend!
goodness Güte, die
gossip Klatsch, der
government Regierung, die
grandad Opa, der
granddaughter Enkelin, die
grandfather Großvater, der
grandmother Großmutter, die
grandson Enkel, der
grannie Oma, die
great groß
greenspace Park, der
guy Typ, der

H

half halb; Hälfte, die
hand Hand, die
happen, to vorkommen
happy, to be froh sein
has to (he/she/it) muss (er/sie/es)
Have a good trip! Gute Reise!
have, to haben
have to, to müssen
head Kopf, der
health Gesundheit, die
hear, to hören
heart Herz, das
heavy schwer
Hello! Hallo!; Guten Tag!
help, to helfen
here hier
hike, to wandern
history Geschichte, die
hole Loch, das
holy heilig
horse Pferd, das
host, -ess Gastgeber(in), der (die)
hot heiß
hotel Hotel, das
hour Stunde, die
house Haus, das
how? wie?
how are you? wie geht's?
how much? wie viel?
human being Mensch, der
hurry, in a eilig
hurt, to schmerzen; wehtun
husband Ehemann, der

I

ice Eis, das
idea Idee, die
if wenn; ob
immediately sofort
in in
in case falls
in English/German auf Englisch/Deutsch
in good time rechtzeitig
in the morning morgens
information Auskunft, die
infront vor
inn Gasthaus, das
inside drinnen
insurance Versicherung, die
into in
is (he, she, it) ist (er, sie, es)
island Insel, die
it doesn't matter es macht nichts
it tastes good das schmeckt gut

J & K

joke Witz, der

jolly munter
journey Fahrt, die
juice Saft, der
jump, to springen
key Schlüssel,der
kindness Güte, die
kiss Kuss, der
kitchen Küche, die
knife Messer, das
know, to kennen; wissen

L

Ladies (toilet) Damen(-toilette)
lady Dame, die
lake See, der
lamp Lampe, die
land Land, das
large groß
last letzte
late spät
laugh, to lachen
leave, to verlassen
left, to the left links, nach links
leg Bein, das
letter Brief, der
library Bibliothek, die
lie, to (e.g. not stand) liegen
life Leben, das
light Licht, das
like wie
like, to mögen
little, a little wenig, ein wenig
live, to wohnen
live/be alive, to leben
liver Leber, die
long lang
look for, to suchen
look, to schauen
lose, to verlieren
lost verloren
love, to lieben
luck Glück, das
luggage Gepäck, das
lunch Mittagessen, das
lung Lunge, die

M

magazine Zeitschrift, die
main railway station Hauptbahnhof
make, to machen
man Mann, der
many viele
map Landkarte, die
market Markt, der
married couple Ehepaar, das
matter Sache, die
may (he/she) kann (er/sie)
mealtime Mahlzeit, die
mean, to bedeuten
meant to, to be sollen
meat Fleisch, das
men Männer, die
menu Speisekarte, die
midday Mittag, der
midday meal Mittagessen, das
might (he/she) könnte (er/sie)
milk Milch, die
minute Minute, die
mistake Fehler, der
money Geld, das
monument Denkmal, das
more mehr
morning Morgen, der
most meiste, der/die/das
mother Mutter, die
motorway Autobahn, die
mountain Berg, der
mouth Mund, der
much viel
museum Museum, das
must (he/she) muß (er/sie)
mustard Senf, der
my mein(e)

N

name Name, der
name, to nennen
nationality Staatsangehörigkeit, die
naturally natürlich
near nah
neck Hals, der; Nacken, der
need, to brauchen
never nie(mals)
new neu
newspaper Zeitung, die
nice nett; schön
night Nacht, die
no kein; nein
no one niemand
nobody niemand
none kein
non-smoker Nichtraucher, der
north Norden, der
northern nördlich
not nicht
not yet noch nicht
nothing nichts
now jetzt
nuclear power Kernenergie, die
number Zahl, die

O

occupation Beruf, der
occupied besetzt
occur, to vorkommen
of von
of course natürlich
off ab
offer, to anbieten
often oft
oil Öl, das
O.K! Alles klar!
old alt
old part of town Altstadt, die
holidays Ferien, die; Urlaub, der
on auf, an
on foot zu Fuß
on the contrary sondern
on time pünktlich
once again/more nochmal; noch einmal
only nur
only then erst dann
onto auf
open offen, auf
opera Oper, die
or oder
order Ordnung, die
our unser(e)
out of aus
outside draußen
over über
overnight stay Übernachtung, die

P

package Paket, das
pair Paar, das
palace Palast, der; Schloss, das
paper Papier, das
parcel Paket, das
park Park, der
park, to parken
parking space Parkplatz, der
particular besonders
passport, ID Ausweis, der; Pass, der
pay, to (be)zahlen
peasant Bauer, der
pension Pension, die
people Leute, die
pepper Pfeffer, der
permit, to erlauben
person Mensch, der
petrol (unleaded) Benzin, (bleifreies), das
petrol station Tankstelle, die

photo Foto, das
picture Bild, das
picture postcard Ansichtskarte, die
pig Schwein, das
Pity!, What a pity! Schade!
place Ort, der; Platz, der
place, to setzen
plant Pflanze, die
plate Teller, der
platform Bahnsteig, der
play, to spielen
pleasant angenehm
police Polizei, die
policeman Polizist, der
policewoman Polizistin, die
possible möglich
post Post, die
post office Post, die
postcard Postkarte, die
potatoes Kartoffeln, die
poultry Geflügel, das
pour, to gießen
pregnant schwanger
prepare, to vorbereiten
prescribe, to verschreiben
prescription Rezept, das
present Geschenk, das
presume, to vermuten
pretty schön
profession Beruf, der
promise, to versprechen
pub Kneipe, die
puke up, to kotzen
pull, to ziehen
pullover Pullover, der
punctual pünktlich
pungent scharf
put, to setzen

Q & R

quick schnell
railway Bahn, die
railway station Bahnhof, der
rain Regen, der
rain, to regnen
rather lieber
reach, to erreichen
read, to lesen
ready fertig
really wirklich
recipe Rezept, das
record (music, etc.) Schallplatte, die
recordad delivery Einschreiben, das
refuel, to tanken
remain bleiben
repaet, to wiederholen
repair, to reparieren
report, to berichten
require, to brauchen
reservation (train, etc.) Reservierung
restaurant Restaurant, das
return ticket Rückfahrkarte, die
rib Rippe, die
rice Reis, der
right rechts; richtig
right away sofort
right, to be stimmen
Right you are! Alles klar!
river Fluss, der
riverbank Ufer, das
road Straße, die,
room Zimmer, das
rucksack Rucksack, der
run, to laufen; rennen

S

sad traurig
said gesagt
sail, to segeln
sale Ausverkauf, der
same gleich
sample, to kosten
sand Sand, der
sausage Wurst, die
save, to retten

say, to sagen
schedule Fahrplan, der
school Schule, die
scream, to schreien
sea Meer, das; See, die
second zweite(r)
seeing that da
seek, to suchen
seem, to scheinen
seen gesehen
select, to wählen
set, to setzen
sharp scharf
shine, to scheinen
ship Schiff, das
shirt Hemd, das
shoe Schuh, der
shop Geschäft, das; Laden, der
shore Ufer, das
show, to zeigen
shower (e.g. bath) Dusche, die
shut, to schliessen
sick, to be krank
sight Sehenswürdigkeit, die
sign, to unterschreiben
signature Unterschrift, die
simple einfach
since da
sing, to singen
single (e.g. ticket) einfach
sister Schwester, die
sister-in-law Schwägerin, die
situation Lage, die; Situation, die
ski, to Ski laufen
skin Haut, die
skirt Rock, der
sleep, to schlafen
sleeping-car Schlafwagen, der
slow langsam
small klein
small package Päckchen, das
smoke, to rauchen
snow Schnee, der
so so
soap Seife, die
something etwas
sometimes manchmal
somewhat etwas
song Lied, das
soon bald
sound Ton, der
soup Suppe, die
sour sauer
souvenir Souvenir; Andenken, das
special besonders
spactacles; Brille, die
spoon Löffel, der
square (in a town) Platz, der
stamp Briefmarke, die
start Beginn, der
start, to beginnen
stay, to bleiben
still noch
stomach Magen, der
stone Stein, der
stop (bus, etc.) Haltestelle, die
store Lager, das
storey Stock, der
story Geschichte, die
straight ahead geradeaus
street Straße, die
street map Stadtplan, der
strong stark
student Student(in), der (die)
subway U-Bahn, die
suddenly plötzlich
sugar Zucker, der
sun Sonne, die
supermarket Supermarkt
support, to unterstützen
sure sicher
surname Familienname, der
sweet süß
swim, to baden; schwimmen
swimming baths Schwimmbad, das

T

take, to nehmen
take-off Abflug, der
talk, to reden
tank up, to tanken
taste good, to gut schmecken
taste, to schmecken
taxi Taxi, das
tea Tee, der
teach, to lehren; unterrichten
teacher Lehrer(in), der (die)
telephone Telefon, das
television Fernsehen, das
telex Fernschreiben, das
temperature Temperatur, die
tent Zelt, das
terrible schrecklich
than als
thank, to danken
thanks, thank you danke (schön)
that (relative pronoun) dass
That's right! Das stimmt!
theatre Theater, das
then dann
there da; dort
thereafter danach
there is/are es gibt
thing Sache, die
think, to denken
thirst Durst, der
thirsty durstig
this diese, -r, -s
throat Hals, der
through durch
ticket Fahrkarte, die
ticket counter Fahrkartenschalter
till bis
timetable Fahrplan, der
tired müde
to nach; zu
to lie (not truth) lügen
to the right rechts
to use "du"/"Sie" duzen/siezen
today heute
together zusammen
toilet Toilette, die
toilet paper Toilettenpapier, das
tomorrow morgen
tomorrow morning morgen früh
tone Ton, der
too auch
tooth Zahn, der
toothache Zahnschmerzen, die
tourist office Fremdenverkehrsamt
towel Handtuch, das
town Stadt, die
trade Handel, der
tragedy Unglück, das
train Zug, der
translator Übersetzer(in), der (die)
travel, to reisen
traveller Reisende, der/die
tree Baum, der
trip Fahrt, die
trousers Hose, die
true wahr
trust, to (someone) vertrauen
truth Wahrheit, die
try, to probieren
try on, to (clothes) anprobieren
tube U-Bahn, die

U

uncertain unsicher
uncle Onkel, der
understand, to verstehen
unfortunately leider

university Universität, die
unsafe unsicher
until bis
up to bis
upon auf
urgent dringend; eilig
use, to benutzen

V

vacation Ferien, die
value-for-money preiswert
vegetables Gemüse, das
very sehr
via über
village Dorf, das
visit Besuch, der
visit, to besuchen
voice Stimme, die
vote, to wählen

W

wait, to warten
wake, to wecken
walk, to gehen
wall Mauer, die; Wand, die
want to, to wollen
warm warm
wash, to waschen
watch Uhr, die
watch, to beobachten
wax Wachs, das
way Weg, der
way in Eingang, der
way out Ausgang, der
we wir
weak schwach
wear, to tragen
weather Wetter, das
week Woche, die
weekend Wochenende, das
well gut
West Westen, der
western westlich
what? was?
what kind of ...? was für ein ...?
wheel Rad, das
when als; wenn
when? wann?
whenever wenn
where? wo?
where from? woher?
where to? wohin?
whether ob
which? welche, -r, -s?
white weiß
who? wer?
why? warum?
wife Ehefrau, die
wild wild
will (he/she) wird (er/sie)
window Fenster, das
wine Wein, der
witch Hexe, die
with mit
without ohne
woman Frau, die
work, to arbeiten
write, to schreiben
wrong falsch

Y

year Jahr, das
yellow gelb
yes ja
yesterday gestern
yet doch
young jung
You're welcome! Bitte!; Bitte sehr!
youth hostel Jugendherberge, die

Vocabulary German – English

A

ab from, off
Abend, der evening
abends in the evening
aber but
Abfahrt, die departure
Abflug, der start, take-off
Abteil, das compartment
Adresse, die address
allein alone
alles all, everything
Alles klar! O.K.! Right you are!
als as, when
alt old
Altstadt, die old part of town
an at, on, to
anbieten to offer
Andenken, das souvenir
angeln gehen to go angling/fishing
angenehm pleasant
ankommen to arrive
Ankunft, die arrival
anprobieren to try on (clothes)
Anschluss, der connection
Anschrift, die address
Ansichtskarte picture postcard
antworten to answer
Apfel, der apple
Appetit, der appetite
arbeiten to work
Arm, der arm
Arzneimittel, das drug
Arzt, der doctor
auch also, too
auf on, onto, upon
Auge, das eye
aus from, out of
ausdrücken to express
Ausflug, der excursion
ausfüllen to fill in/out
Ausgang, der exit, way out
Auskunft, die information
Ausländer(in), der (die) foreigner
aussteigen to alight/get out
Ausverkauf, der sale
Ausweis, der passport, ID
Auto, das car
Autobahn, die freeway, motorway

B

Bad, das bath
baden to bathe/swim
Badezimmer, das bathroom
Bäcker, der baker
Bäckerei, die bakery
Bahn, die railway
Bahnhof, der railway station
Bahnsteig, der platform
bald soon
Ball, der ball
Bank, die bank, bench
Bauer, der farmer, peasant
Baum, der tree
bedeuten to mean
beenden to end/finish
Beginn, der beginning, start
beginnen to begin/start
bei at, in
beide, -s both
Bein, das leg
Beispiel, das example
bekommen to get
benutzen to use
Benzin, (bleifreies), das petrol (unleaded)

Vocabulary German – English

beobachten to watch
Berg, der mountain
berichten to report
Berliner Mauer, die Berlin Wall
Beruf, der occupation, profession
besetzt busy, occupied
besonders particular, special
besser better
beste, der/die/das the best
Besuch, der visit
besuchen to visit
Betäubungsmittel, das anaesthetic
Bett, das bed
bevor before
bezahlen to pay
Bibliothek, die library
Bier, das beer
Bild, das picture
billig cheap
bis till, until, up to
bis morgen till tomorrow
Bitte! Bitte sehr! You're welcome!
bitter bitter
blau blue, drunk (colloq.)
bleiben to remain/stay
Blut, das blood
brauchen to need/require
braun brown
brechen to break
Bremse, die brake
Brief, der letter
Briefmarke, die stamp
Brille, die glasses, spectacles
Brötchen, das bread roll
Brot, das bread
Bruder, der brother
Brücke, die bridge
Brust, die breast, chest
Buch, das book
Bundesstraße, die A-road (Br.)
Bus, der bus, coach
Busbahnhof, der bus/coach station
Bushaltestelle, die bus stop
Butter, die butter

C & D

Camping, das camping
Campingplatz, der camping site
Champagner, der champagne
da as, there
damals at that time, then
Dame, die lady
Damen(-toilette) Ladies (toilet)
danach then, thereafter
danke (schön) thanks, thank you
danken to thank
dann afterwards, then
dürfen to be allowed
dass that (relative pronoun)
Daten, die data
Datum, das date
denken to think
Denkmal, das monument
Deutsch, deutsch German
diese, r, -s this
doch after all, but
Dorf, das village
dort there
draußen outside
dringend urgent
drinnen inside
durch through
Durst, der thirst
durstig thirsty
Dusche, die shower (i.e. as in bath)
duzen to use "du"

E

Ecke, die corner
Ehefrau, die wife
Eheman, der husband
Ehepaar, das married couple
Ei, das egg
eilig in a hurry, urgent
Eilzustellung, die express delivery
ein wenig a little
einfach simple
Eingang, der entrance, way in
Einschreiben, das certified letter, recorded delivery
einsteigen to climb/get in
Eis, das ice
Ende, das end
Englisch English
Englisch, auf in English
Enkel, der grandson
Enkelin, die granddaughter
entkommen to escape
entweder ... oder either ... or
erbrechen to vomit
Erde, die earth
erklären to declare/explain
erlauben to allow/permit
erreichen to achieve/reach
erste(r) first
erst only
erst dann only then
es gibt there is/are
es macht nichts it doesn't matter
es schmeckt gut it tastes good
essen to eat
Etage, die floor
etwa about, approximately
etwas something, somewhat

F

Fähre, die ferry
fahren to drive/go
Fahrkarte, die ticket
Fahrkartenschalter, der - ticket counter
Fahrplan, der timetable, schedule
Fahrrad, das bicycle
Fahrt, die journey, trip
falls in case, if
falsch false, wrong
Familienname, der surname
Fax, das fax
Fehler, der mistake
Feld, das field
Fenster, das window
Ferien, die vacation
Ferien, die holidays
Fernschreiben, das telex
Fernsehen, das television
Fernsprecher, der telephone
fertig finished, ready
Feuer, das fire
Fieber, das fever, temperature
finden to find
Finger, der finger
Fisch, der fish
Flasche, die bottle
Fleisch, das meat
fliegen to fly
Flughafen, der airport
Flugzeug, das aircraft
Fluss, der river
folgen to follow
Formular, das form
Foto das photo(graph)
Fotograf, der photographer
Frankreich France
Französisch French
Frau, die lady, wife, woman
frei free

Vocabulary German – English

Freiheit, die freedom
freilich of course!
Fremdenverkehrsamt, das tourist office
Freund, der (boy-)friend
Freundin, die (girl-)friend
freundlich friendly
froh sein to be happy
Frost, der frost
früh early
Frühstück, das breakfast
Führerschein, der driving licence
für for
Fuß, der foot
Fußball, der football

G

Gabel, die fork
Gastgeber(in), der (die) host(ess)
Gasthaus, das hotel, inn
Gaststätte, die pub, restaurant
Gebäude, das building
geben to give
gefällt es dir/Ihnen? do you like it?
Geflügel, das poultry
gehen to go/walk
gelb yellow
Geld, das money
Gemüse, das vegetables
genug enough
geöffnet open
Gepäck, das luggage
geradeaus straight ahead
Gericht, das dish, court (of law)
Geschäft, das business, shop
Geschenk, das gift, present
Geschichte, die history, story
geschlossen closed
Geschwister, die brothers and sisters
Gespräch, das conversation
gestern yesterday
Gesundheit! Bless you! (after sneezing)
Gesundheit, die health
gießen to cast/pour
gleich at once, same
Glück, das luck
Gott, der God
Grenze, die border, frontier
groß big, great, large
Großmutter, die grandmother
Großvater, der grandfather
Grünanlage, die park
Güte, die goodness, kindness
gut good, well
gut schmecken to taste good
Gute Reise! Have a good trip!
guten Abend good evening
guten Appetit enjoy your meal
Guten Tag Hello!

H

Haare, die hair
haben to have
halb half
Hälfte, die half
Hals, der neck, throat
Haltestelle, die stop (bus, etc.)
Hand, die hand
Handel, der trade
Handtuch, das towel
Hauptbahnhof, der main railway station
Haus, das house
Haut, die skin
heilig holy
heiß hot
heißen to call

helfen to help
Hemd, das shirt
Herz, das heart
heute today
Hexe, die witch
hier here
hören to hear
Hose, die trousers
Hotel, das hotel
Huhn, das chicken
Hund, der dog

I & J

ich möchte I'd like
Idee, die idea
immer always
in in, into
Insel, die island
Irrtum, der error
ja yes
Jahr, das year
jede, -r, -s each, every
jetzt now
Jugendherberge, die youth hostel
jung young
Junge, der boy

K

Kaffee, der coffee
kalt cold
Kamm, der comb
kaputt broken, busted
Karte, die map
Kartoffeln, die potatoes
Kassette, die cassette
Katze, die cat
kaufen to buy
kein no, none
kennen to know
kennen lernen to get to know (s.o.)
Kern, der core
Kernenergie, die nuclear power
Kind, das child
Kino, das cinema
Klamotten, die clothes (colloq.)
Klatsch, der gossip
Kleid, das dress (for ladies)
Kleidung, die clothes
klein small
können to be able to
kommen to come
Konzert, das concert
Kopf, der head
kosten to cost (price, etc.), to try
kotzen to puke up
Kuchen, der cake
Küche, die kitchen
Kuss, der kiss

L

lachen to laugh
Laden, der shop
Lage, die situation
Lager, das camp, store
Lampe, die lamp
Land, das country, land
Landkarte, die map
lang long
langsam slow
laufen to run
leben to be alive/live
Leben, das life
Lebensmittel food
Lebensmittelgeschäft, das food shop
Leber, die liver
lecker delicious
lehren to teach
Lehrer(in), der (die) teacher
leider unfortunately
lesen to read
letzte(r) last
Leute, die people

Licht, das light
lieben to love
lieber rather
Lied, das song
liegen to lie (i.e. not stand)
links, nach links left, to the left
Loch, das hole
Löffel, der spoon
Los! come on!, get going!
lügen to lie (not truth)
Luft, die air
Luftpost, die airmail
Lunge, die lung
Lust, die desire

M

machen to make
Mädchen, das girl
Magen, der stomach
manchmal sometimes
Mann, der husband, man
Markt, der market
Mauer, die wall
Meer, das sea
mehr more
mein(e) my, mine
meiste (der/die/das) most**Mensch, der** human being, person
Messer, das knife
Milch, die milk
Minute, die minute
mit with
Mittag, der lunch-break, midday
Mittagessen, das lunch, midday meal
mittags at lunchtime
mögen to like/want
morgen tomorrow
Morgen, der morning
morgen früh tomorrow morning
morgens in the morning
müde tired
müssen to have to
Mund, der mouth
munter cheerful, jolly
Museum, das museum
Mutter, die mother

N

nach after, to
Nacht, die night
nachts at night
Nacken, der neck (back of)
nah near
Name, der name
natürlich naturally, of course
nehmen to take
nein no
nennen to name
nett nice
neu new
nicht not
Nichtraucher, der non-smoker
nichts nothing
nie(mals) never
niemand no one, nobody
noch still
noch (ein)mal once again, once more
noch nicht not yet
nördlich northern
Norden, der north
nur only

O

ob if, whether
Obst, das fruit
oder or
Öl, das oil
östlich eastern
offen open
oft often
ohne without

Ohr, das ear
Oma, die grannie
Onkel, der uncle
Opa, der grandad
Oper, die opera
Ordnung, die order
Ort, der place
Osten, der East
Ostern Easter

P

Paar, das couple, pair
Päckchen, das small package
Paket, das package, parcel
Palast, der palace
Panne, die breakdown (car)
Papier, das paper
Park, der greenspace, park
parken to park
Parkplatz, der parking space
Pass, der passport, ID
Pech, das bad luck
Pension, die cheap hotel, pension
Pfeffer, der pepper
Pferd, das horse
Pflanze, die plant
Pflicht, die duty
Platz, der place, square
Platzkarte, die reservation (train, etc.)
plötzlich suddenly
plombieren to fill (teeth)
Polizei, die police
Polizist, der policeman
Polizistin, die policewoman
Pommes frites, die chips; fries
Post, die post
Postamt, das post office
Postkarte, die postcard
preiswert value-for-money
probieren to try
pünktlich on time, punctual
Pullover, der pullover

R

Rad, das bicycle, wheel
rauchen to smoke
rechts right, to the right
rechtzeitig in good time
reden to talk
Regen, der rain
Regierung, die government
regnen to rain
Reis, der rice
reisen to travel
Reisende (der/die) traveller
rennen to run
reparieren to repair
Restaurant, das restaurant
retten to save
Rezept, das prescription, recipe
richtig correct, right
Rippe, die rib
Rock, der skirt
Rucksack, der rucksack
Rückfahrkarte, die return ticket

S

Sache, die thing, affair
Saft, der juice
sagen to say
Sahne, die cream
Sand, der sand
sauber clean
Sauberkeit, die cleanliness
sauer angry, sour
Schade! Pity!, What a pity!
Schallplatte, die record (i.e. music)

Vocabulary German – English

scharf pungent, sharp
schauen to look, to look (at)
scheinen to seem, shine
schenken to give (a present)
Schiff, das ship
schlafen to sleep
Schlafwagen, der sleeping-car
schlecht bad
schliessen to close/shut
Schloss, das castle, palace
Schlüssel, der key
schmecken to taste
schmerzen to hurt
Schnee, der snow
schnell fast, quick
schön beautiful, nice, pretty
Schokolade, die chocolate
schon already
schrecklich terrible
schreiben to write
schreien to scream
Schuh, der shoe
Schule, die school
schwach weak
Schwägerin, die sister-in-law
Schwager, der brother-in-law
schwanger pregnant
schwarz black
Schwein, das pig
schwer heavy
Schwester, die sister
schwierig difficult
Schwimmbad, das swimming baths
schwimmen to swim
See, der lake
See, die sea
segeln to sail
Sehenswürdigkeit, die sight
sehr very
Seife, die soap
sein to be
Sekt, der German champagne
Semmel, die bread roll
Senf, der mustard
setzen to put, to set
sicher certain, sure
siezen to use "Sie"
singen to sing
Situation, die situation
Ski laufen to ski
so as, so
sofort immediately, right away
sollen to be meant to
sondern but, on the contrary
Sonne, die sun
Souvenir, das souvenir
so ... wie as ... as
spät late
spazieren gehen to go for a walk
Speisekarte, die menu
Speisewagen, der dining car
Spiel, das game
spielen to play
springen to jump
Staatsangehörigkeit, die nationality
Stadt, die city, town
Stadtplan, der street map
stark strong
Stein, der stone
Stelle, die place
Stimme, die voice
stimmen to be right
Stock, der storey
Stockwerk, das floor
Strand, der beach
Straße, die road, street
Student(in), der (die) student
Stunde, die hour
suchen to look for, to seek
süß sweet
Supermarkt supermarket
Suppe, die soup

T

täglich daily
Tag, der day
tagsüber during the day
tanken to refuel, to tank up
Tankstelle, die gas/petrol station
Tante, die aunt
Tanz, der dance
tanzen to dance
Tasse, die cup
Taxi, das taxi
Tee, der tea
Telefon, das telephone
Teller, der plate
teuer expensive
Theater, das theatre
Tier, das animal
Tod, der death
Toilette, die toilet
Toilettenpapier, das toilet paper
Ton, der sound, tone
Torte, die cake
tot dead
tragen to carry, to wear
traurig sad
Trinkwasser, das drinking water
trocken dry
Tschüss! Bye!
Tür, die door
Typ, der bloke, guy

U

U-Bahn, die tube, subway
über about, above
Übernachtung, die overnight stay
Übersetzer(in), der (die) translator
Uhr, die clock, watch
Umleitung, die diversion
umsteigen to change (trains, etc.)
und and
Unfall, der accident
Unglück, das accident, disaster
Universität, die university
unser(e) our
unsicher uncertain, unsafe
unterrichten to teach
unterschreiben to sign
Unterschrift, die signature
unterstützen to support
Urlaub, der holidays
Ursache, die cause

V

Vater, der father
vergleichen to compare
verlassen to abandon/leave
verlieren to lose
verloren lost
vermuten to assume/presume
verrückt crazy
verschreiben to prescribe
Versicherung, die insurance
Verspätung, die delay
versprechen to promise
verstehen to understand
vertrauen to trust (someone)
viel much
viele many
von from, of
vor before, in front
vor (zwei Tagen) (two days) ago
vorbereiten to prepare
vorkommen to happen/occur

Vocabulary German – English

W

Wachs, der wax
wählen to choose/select
Wagen, der car
wahr true
Wahrheit, die truth
Wald, der forest
Wand, die wall
wandern to hike
wann? when?
warm warm
warten to wait
warum? why?
was? what?
was für ein …? what kind of …?
waschen to wash
wechseln to change (e.g. monoey)
Wechselstube, die exchange office
wecken to wake
Weg, der road, way
wehtun to hurt
Weihnachten Christmas
weil because
Wein, der wine
weiß white
weit far
welche, -r, -s ? which?
wenig little
wenn if, when
wer? who?
werden to become
Westen, der West
westlich western
Wetter, das weather
wie like
wie? how?
wie geht's? how are you?
wiederholen to repeat
wie viel? how much?
wild wild
Wild, das game (i.e. meat)
wirklich really
Wirtschaft, die economy
wissen to know
Witz, der joke
wo? where?
Woche, die week
Wochenende, das weekend
Wörterbuch, das dictionary
woher? where from?
wohin? where to?
wohnen to live
Wolke, die cloud
wollen to want to
wütend angry
Wurst, die sausage

Z

zählen to count
Zahl, die number
zahlen to pay
Zahn, der tooth
Zahnschmerzen, die toothache
zeigen to show
Zeitschrift, die magazine
Zeitung, die newspaper
Zelt, das tent
ziehen to draw/pull
Zigarette, die cigarette
Zimmer, das room
zu at, closed, to
zu Fuß on foot
zu Hause at home
Zucker, der sugar
Zug, der train
zum Beispiel (z.B.) for example (e.g.)
zusammen together

Kauderwelsch

This book in other languages

Allemand (in French)
ISBN 978-3-89416-329-7
CD: 978-3-8317-6228-6

Alemán (in Spanish)
ISBN 978-3-89416-358-7
CD: 978-3-8317-6104-3

Niemiecki (in Polish)
ISBN 978-3-89416-359-4
CD: 978-3-8317-6108-1

Német (in Hungarian)
ISBN 978-3-89416-469-0
CD: 978-3-8317-6107-4

Almanca (in Turkish)
ISBN 978-3-89416-744-8
CD: 978-3-8317-6229-3

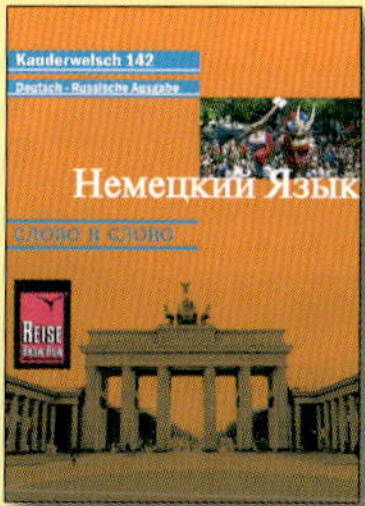

Nemeckij (in Russian)
ISBN 9783-89416-511-6
CD: 978-3-8317-6045-9

Reise Know-How Verlag, Bielefeld
www.reise-know-how.de

Learn German with no sweat!
KAUDERWELSCH German Pronunciation Trainer
The PRONUNCIATION TRAINER makes the most important phrases and expressions from the conversation section of the Kauderwelsch book (marked with an) audible from CD: with pauses for you to repeat and keep in mind what you've heard.
● Price: € 7,90 [D]
● ISBN: 978-3-8317-6040-4
www.reise-know-how.de

The author

Bob Ordish, born near London in 1954, lived and worked as a translator in West Germany from 1983 to 1989 (Mainz and Frankfurt). In the 1970s he also taught English near Hamburg, spent time at Heidelberg and Gießen and has travelled extensivly in the other German speaking countries.

In 1980 he obtained a degree in German from London University, but says that "a degree itself doesn't prove you can actually speak the language. The only way to do that is to go to the country, talk and not be afraid of making mistakes".

Besides translating, his work experience in Germany (and Britain) takes in such diverse areas as banking, chemicals, production lines, building sites, hotels, van-driving.
Bob Ordish died in 2001.